The
Book of
Spells

The
Book of
Spells

Powerful Magic To Make Your Dreams Come True

Pamela Ball

All images courtesy of Shutterstock.

This edition published in 2021 by Arcturus Publishing Limited
26/27 Bickels Yard, 151–153 Bermondsey Street,
London SE1 3HA

AD007732UK

Printed in the UK

An it harm none...

These words are the first part of the Wiccan Rede, the statement that is the basis for the key moral system in Wicca and certain other forms of witchcraft. The remainder of the statement is 'Do what thou wilt', and most interpret it to imply the belief that the spirit of the Rede is to actively do good for one's fellow humans as well as for oneself.

Lest we be accused of undue influence, as have others before us, we hereby take responsibility for the words written within the pages of this book. We do not, however, take any responsibility for your performance of the spells and rituals herein nor for the results of the use of the Powers. Such performance and result is a transaction between you and those Powers, for which you yourself must take responsibility.

We trust that this book will help you in your search for understanding and offer a blessing to help you on your way:

May the Divine be with you.
May you always be guided, guarded and protected.

Contents

Introduction

The desire to change and improve that which we have has been around for many thousands of years, if not since man first walked the earth. Magic and spell-working have always been a part of that, and indeed still are today. Anyone who practises any form of magic, including spell-working, needs to be grounded. This means having both feet firmly planted in reality and also having a basic knowledge of what magic is and is not, what spells can and can't do, and what – with practice – you can do with the tools, information and knowledge you have. This book sets out to give you that information in as succinct a manner as possible.

It is sometimes best not to attempt any definition of ancient magic and magical belief. However, in any discussion of magic and its practitioners we must take account of a period in which the magical traditions of several different cultures coalesced and merged into a type of international and even multicultural magical practice, with its own rituals, symbols and words of power. This occurred in the Mediterranean basin and the Near East from the 1st to the 7th centuries AD and is the basis of most of the early, more intellectually based, systems of magic.

The pursuit of magic is, in part, the result of the human desire for control. In this period there was a need to control the natural environment, the social world, and the outcome of those forces we did not fully understand. This underlying desire for control comes to the surface most often in times of change, as we have seen repeatedly over the last fifteen centuries. During this time the techniques may have been modified, but the goals have remained the same. The basic laws of magic, of control, still apply today just as they have always done.

Curiosity, exploration and secrecy

One of most interesting characters from early times was Abraham Abulafia (1240–95), who made available much arcane knowledge, which ultimately formed the basis of Kabbalah. Believing in the divine nature of the Hebrew alphabet, he held that God cannot be described or conceptualized using everyday symbols. He therefore used abstract letter combinations and permutations *(tzeruf)* in intense meditations lasting for hours to reach ecstatic states.

These were spells in the real sense of the word since they literally 'spelt out' the keys to altered states of consciousness – failure to carry through the keys correctly could have a far-reaching effect on the careless practitioner, resulting in madness and other states of illusion. Again, these beliefs have been brought through to the modern day and used to great effect. Controlled use of altered states of consciousness, backed up by empirical evidence, is still one of the most potent tools a magical practitioner or spell-worker can have.

The Renaissance period in Europe saw the coming to prominence of many secret societies and scholar-magicians. Because of the burgeoning natural curiosity encouraged by Renaissance principles, a new importance was placed on the actual controlling of the forces of nature. The basis of magic-working had previously been seen as harnessing the power of spirits and demons. Now, additionally, the human mind was a factor to be considered and magical working was geared to gaining power, not only over external forces but also over internal states. Much good work was done in understanding the interaction between the spiritual realm and the physical, and how changes can be brought about within the latter. Both Kabbalah and alchemy, one of whose objectives was to transform baser metals into gold, became very popular.

By the 17th century, folk magic and witchcraft were being used side by side, often with little differentiation between them. Most people were alternately fascinated and frightened by energies that offered control of nature coupled with opportunities for enormous wealth. However, witchcraft then became more widely identified with demonic or satanic entities opposed to God and therefore was deemed to be wholly evil. A heretic was defined as a traitor – an offence punishable by death – and the persecution of those who did not conform to the so-called religious thought of the day became relentless. This caused the practice of witchcraft to go underground not just in terms of secrecy but in actuality, for example in the use of caves and secret places, such as Wookey Hole in Somerset, England.

The practice of magic survived however and by the 19th century there is evidence that many secret societies, each surrounded by its own unique mysteries, still survived. They were often formed by highly creative people who were searching for new and different ways of self-expression. Many of the beliefs of these societies were based on the old traditions, though some differed widely from those of the old alchemists. Rituals and invocations were developed that were supposedly based on the ancient rites, often with a very strong bias towards melodrama. Secret societies have also survived into the present day, though not always with full awareness of the fact that their rituals are based on magical practice.

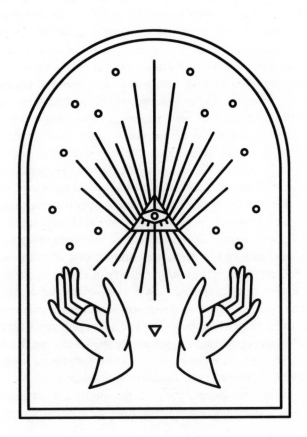

Modern magic

Today there is a rich heritage of magical practices and beliefs on which we can call to satisfy our need for control over our own lives. Where conventional religion no longer offers an outlet for our sense of belonging, we can turn to magical rituals and spell-making to honour our origins. We can make use of the knowledge and practices that have been handed down to us and have survived, often in the face of adversity. The principles that form the basis of magical practice still operate today, as do the various belief systems associated with them.

Many of these belief systems take their names from the Greek word *theo,* meaning god. One can be polytheistic (belief in many gods) yet see all things as being part of one great mystery, or monotheistic (belief in one god) yet recognize that for others there may be many gods. Then again, one might be an atheist (with no belief in god) and yet retain a simple belief in one's own power.

In the working of magical spells no one can tell you what to believe – you must make your own decisions. The words 'paganism' and 'pagan' come from the Latin *paganus,* meaning 'rustic' or 'belonging to the country'. Largely, ancient paganism was pantheistic (believing in all gods) but today the word has come to mean someone who does not recognize the God of the main religions of the world, such as Christianity or Judaism. We are much closer to a belief in the power of nature and for those who seek to use magic and spell-making in their daily lives, there is the need for love and respect for all living things. How we express that will be mirrored in our spell-making.

Spell-making is such an individual craft that nobody can, or indeed should, be so bold as to try to tell others how to cast their spells. However, in some areas it is useful to receive guidance as a starting point from which you can devise your own ways of working. This book is divided into two parts; in the first we look at what you will need to begin working with spells. This includes the tools you will need, how to create sacred space, and the best way to set up for spell-working. Finally, in this first section, we advise on the best ways for constructing your spell and rituals and how to record your methods and results.

The spells in the second part of the book are divided into the following four categories: Friendship, Love and Relationships; Health,

Healing and Well-being; Money, Luck and Career; Home and Personal Protection. As such, the spells contained here cover most instances in which magic might be required.

Each spell has an introductory paragraph with information as to what type of spell it is, the best time to carry it out, and which discipline it comes from (if known). We then tell you what you will need and then give you the method to use. Some spells require incantations, some invocations and others simple actions to make them work, and this is laid out for you.

If a spell doesn't work for you in the way that we have suggested, it might be that your intended result does not fit into the overall scheme of things. Do try it again on another occasion and use your intuition to decide what might be changed or adjusted to suit your personality. Have confidence in yourself and never be afraid to experiment.

Popular acceptance of magical powers and spell-making will always be mixed. Some people will accept unquestioningly, others will search for alternative causes and others still will remain concerned by the manifestation of such powers. For some people these powers are part of everyday life and it is for each individual to decide whether or not they wish to develop and use them.

It now merely remains for us to wish you health, wealth and happiness and the hope that you enjoy your spell-work and its results!

Part 1

THE
TOOLS

What will I need?

When performing your spells and magical workings, you will find that you need to understand why you use certain tools in specific ways. Before learning how to set up your altar (see page 82), here is a list of the most commonly used tools.

Altar Objects
This is a general term for the objects that you place on your altar – candleholders, flower vases, crystals and so forth – which do not necessarily have a specific magical use of their own; they are present to create an ambience. You should remember to dedicate them to the purpose in hand by presenting them to your chosen deity, ancestor or guiding spirit.

Athame
By tradition, the athame is a ceremonial knife used especially in the performing of spells. It is not intended for cutting herbs and so on: its role is ceremonial, for example indicating the quarters or directions. Ideally it should be of the best and purest metal available. Its handle is usually black and sometimes carved with magical designs and symbols. Many experienced magical practitioners consider that the most powerful athame is one which has been inherited.

Besom
A besom is a different name for a broom, and is particularly associated with the easily recognizable so-called 'witch's broom' of old. It is a particularly personal tool, and is often made specially for the practitioner, with twigs from the tree of her choice. It is usually kept specifically to be used in the sacred space or circle – this time for cleansing – and is also used both symbolically and spiritually.

Boline
The boline is a knife traditionally used in cutting plants, herbs, wands and other objects for spells and other magical workings. It is akin to the gardener's pruning knife as a useful, practical tool. It often has a white handle and a curved blade. It is consecrated because this is a way of honouring its purpose as a magical tool.

Burin

A burin is a sharp-pointed instrument used for inscribing candles and other magical objects with symbols, words and pictures in order to make spells more effective. In many ways, it is more effective than either the boline or the athame and is used much more as an instrument which pierces a surface rather than cuts it.

Candles

Candles are such an integral part of a spell-maker's work that they have become a whole branch of magic all their own. They represent the Element of Fire, but also light. Various colours bring different things to magical workings and they are an important part of any ritual (see pages 21-29).

Cauldron

Because cauldrons were easily disguised as cooking utensils in olden days, most people today tend to think of them as a large cast-iron pot. There has lately been a return to original materials and nowadays they can be made of almost anything. They are often of a size that can be stood on the altar, or in the sacred space. They are used mainly as containers for herbs, candles and other magical objects.

Chalice

Used as a ceremonial drinking vessel, the chalice is sometimes made from precious metal, although it can also be made from glass. An elegant object, the chalice will usually be beautifully decorated with elaborate designs that may have magical significance.

Charcoal

Charcoal is a component of incense and oil burning. Nowadays, the best charcoal is usually found in compressed small discs of about 3 cm (1 inch). These give a burning time of approximately 45 minutes.

Compass

While this may seem a somewhat unusual tool, many spells, rituals and techniques require that you honour or face certain directions or compass points in their performance. It is also necessary to know the correct alignment in Feng Shui. Much the easiest way to work out the directions is by using a compass. It does not need to be particularly decorative, ornate or expensive, merely one with which you are happy to work.

Incense and Oil Burner

The choice of this tool must be a personal matter. An incense burner should give plenty of room to allow the aromas and smoke to disperse properly. Traditional material such as brass or clay may be used. The best shape is slightly flat rather than too concave. Oil burners should be of a sufficient size to allow a long enough time to complete your spell. Burners which allow you to float the oil on water, which then evaporates, are probably the safest.

Paper

During spells you will often need to write your wishes or aims down and it is good to have some paper ready prepared. Parchment type is best, but heavier good quality is perfectly acceptable. You consecrate it by holding it for a short period in the smoke from your favourite incense.

Pen and Ink

Traditionally, quill pens were used for writing spells and incantations, but if you can't find a quill then use the best pen you can afford. Try to keep it especially for magical work and consecrate it by passing it carefully over the top of a candle or through incense. Also buy a good-quality ink and, if not already formulated for magical purposes, consecrate that in the same way. Neither pen nor ink should be used for other purposes.

Pentacle

The pentacle is a shallow dish, which is usually inscribed with a pentagram – a five-pointed star. It is used as a 'power point' for consecrating other objects such as water or wine in a chalice, amulets and tools.

Pestle and Mortar

The pestle and mortar are so symbolic of the union of God and Goddess that they deserve a special mention within the use of magical tools. Mainly used to prepare herbal mixtures and incenses, they can also become part of your altar furniture when consecrated.

Scrying Tools

Scrying is the practice of using certain channelling tools, which should be consecrated before use – such as crystals, mirrors, coloured water, runes and so forth – to try to gain an insight into external events. Any object can be used for scrying, though usually they are reflective, and they employ the arts of concentration and contemplation.

Staff

The staff is used very frequently by practitioners today, particularly if they are of the Druidic persuasion. Longer than the wand, it has the same attributes and uses. A staff is deliberately fashioned for the practitioner from wood taken from sacred trees, such as oak, hawthorn and hazelnut.

Wand

The wand should be no longer than the forearm and is often made from sacred wood. Since the wand is a very personal object, it should be chosen carefully and equally carefully attuned to your own energies. It cannot be used magically until it has been consecrated.

Obviously, you will not need to use all of your tools all of the time and you should develop for yourself some way of storing them, so that they retain their potency. You can do this by perhaps keeping them on your altar or in your sacred space. Use a specially dedicated box or other container or, if you know they are not likely to be interfered with, simply wrapped in black silk or velvet. Treat your tools with respect and they will serve you well.

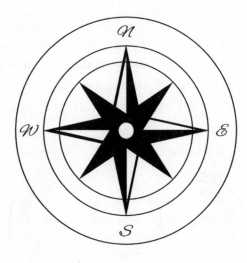

Components of Magical Working

Just as a recipe contains ingredients, so there are certain components that are needed in magical workings, in order to enhance the power and energy that is created. To the uninitiated some of these may seem strange, yet if we remember that much magic initially had to be performed with only what was immediately and easily available to the practitioner, the use of such items makes a great deal of sense. Candles, herbs, oils and so on thus become an important part of modern-day spell-working.

CANDLES
....

Candles should be chosen carefully with regard to type, and colour, depending on the purpose of the spell. It is often better to use your intuition when choosing the type of candle, although for ease of reference, below is a list of the principal types. There are other types available, but these are the most suitable for magical working.

Table
The most readily available candle, these are ideal for many of the spells in this book. They usually burn for six to eight hours and need to be properly seated in suitable candlesticks. All colours can be used, but they should not be dipped, except in exceptional circumstances, and should be of the best quality possible. It is sensible to keep a ready supply at hand.

Pillar
This is a free-standing candle. It is usually in the form of a simple pillar, although it can sometimes be made in other shapes which can be used as part of the spell, for example heart shapes for love spells. This type of candle is best burned on a flat holder since it usually takes some time to burn out.

Taper
These candles are tall and thin and need a particularly stable candle-holder. They are either made in a mould, or by the traditional method of dipping a length of wick into hot molten white or coloured wax. For magical purposes they should be coloured all the way through. They can often be used when a quick result is required. They are quite fragile so you need to be careful not to break them when anointing them.

Tea lights
These small candles are excellent for use when a candle must be left to burn out, but are less easy to anoint with essential oils. Poured in metal pots like small votives, they are normally used in oil burners or specially-made tea-light holders. Depending on their size, they usually burn for approximately four hours.

Votive

This type of candle is specially designed as an offering, to carry prayers to whichever deity you honour. As the wax melts, the holder, which is made of glass, can become hot so some care must be taken when using them. They are designed to be long-burning, usually between one and seven days.

Choosing your candles

There are several things you need to remember when choosing a candle:

1. Choose your candle type as above.
2. Candles used for magic should always be virgin (unused) at the start of the working, unless you have deliberately cleared them of past influences. Using candles that have been previously lit can have a detrimental effect on your spell. They may have picked up influences from previous use.
3. Charge your candle before using it. This can be done by anointing it with oils associated with the magic you intend on performing, or by simply touching it and filling it with your own energy.
4. The oils used in the anointing of your candle should, where possible, always be natural fragrances. While charging the candle, smooth from top to bottom when drawing energy toward you, bottom to top when sending energy outwards. Particularly when anointing candles for altar use, anoint from the middle to the top and from the middle to the bottom to signify the union of spiritual and physical realms.
5. If you enjoy craftwork, it is a very good idea to make your own candles for magical use. It is a whole art in itself – you infuse your candles with your own energy and thus increase the magical potency of the candle many times over. It is relatively easy to make your own candles: simply heat the wax until it is liquid and pour into a mould which is threaded with a wick. The wax should now be left to cool, after which the mould can be removed. Oils and colours can be added for extra potency.

Dressing and charging candles

Dressing (anointing) and charging candles are perhaps candle magic in its simplest form. Dressing a candle performs two functions. By anointing it with oil you ensure that it burns safely and you also have the opportunity to infuse it with the required vibration for your working. Charging a candle ensures you fix the intent of your magical working and also dedicates the candle to the appropriate purpose.

Dressing Candles

Any oil can be used for dressing a candle but initially it is best to use either your favourite essential oil, such as frankincense, or perhaps an oil infused with a suitable herb appropriate to the task in hand. (A list of popular oils suitable for various purposes is given on pages 72-75.)

There are various ways to dress a candle but what is important is the direction in which you anoint it. If you remember that working from the top down draws in power from spiritual sources, and working from the bottom up draws in energy from the earth, it is very easy to work correctly for your purpose. Never rub across the whole candle with a back and forth movement, as you will end up with a confusion of energies – not to say a sputtering candle.

YOU WILL NEED
Candle
Oil

METHOD
Sit quietly and, holding the candle, think carefully about your intent. If you have learned to meditate, then enter a meditative state and allow the energies to build up within you.

To bring something to you, rub oil on the candle in a downward motion from the top to the middle and then from the bottom to the middle.

To send something away from you, you rub the oil from the middle of the candle out to the ends.

Continue with either movement until you have a sense that you have done enough. If you have any oil left on your hands either rub your hands together until the oil is absorbed or dab the remaining oil from your fingers onto the centre of your forehead, which is the Third Eye and the seat of vision. Then say the following or something similar:

I cleanse and consecrate this candle

(in the name of your chosen deity if you choose to recognise one). May it burn with strength in the service of the Greater Good.

Your candle is now ready for use.

Charging Candles

This is a quick, uncomplicated method of more fully charging a candle. This method can be used without having to set up your altar completely. It can equally be used to charge your altar candles.

YOU WILL NEED

A candle or candles of the appropriate colour
(if preferred, mark them with appropriate symbols)
A candle holder
Matches rather than a lighter

METHOD

Hold the candle in your 'power hand' (the hand you consider you give out energy with).

Open the other hand and turn that palm towards the sky. Breathe deeply and visualize your goal.

Now perceive whatever you think of as Universal Energy flowing through the palm that is turned skyward, filling your body.

Visualise that Universal Energy mixing within you with the energy of your intention.

Now allow that mixed energy to flow into the candle. Be conscious of the energy as it builds up.

Feel the energy streaming into the candle.

Fill it from bottom to top as though the candle were an empty vessel.

If you are comfortable with doing so, speak your intention out loud.

As you place the candle in its holder, stabilize the thought within the candle so that it will be converted into pure clear intent.

Strike a match above the candle.

Draw down the flame toward the candle, lighting the wick.

Extinguish the match flame, but do not blow it out in case you blow out the candle.

Stay with the candle for a few moments visualizing your intention, feeling its energy moving into the universe.

Leave the area and let the candle burn right down as it does its work.

Candle colour and the symbols inscribed on them create additional power. As you become more proficient, you will find yourself using certain colours and symbols more often. Try not to be too rigid, and always be open to widening your focus.

Candle colours

Many different colours are used in candle magic and below are listed the most common ones, along with their key associations and purposes. You may not wish to use black candles because of their association with the darker side of magic. If so, dark grey is a good substitute. White can be used as a substitute if your chosen colour is not available.

White
• The Goddess
• Higher Self
• Purity
• Peace
• Virginity

Black
• Binding
• Shape shifting
• Protection
• Repels negativity

Brown
• Special favours
• To influence friendships
• Healing earth energies

Orange
• General success
• Property deals
• Legal matters
• Justice
• Selling

Purple
• Third eye
• Psychic ability
• Hidden knowledge
• To influence people in high places
• Spiritual power

Blue
- The Element of Water
- Wisdom
- Protection
- Calm
- Good fortune
- Opening communication
- Spiritual inspiration

Pink
- Affection
- Romance
- Caring
- Nurturing
- Care for the planet earth

Green
- The Element of Earth
- Physical healing
- Monetary success
- Mother Earth
- Tree and plant magic
- Growth
- Personal goals

Red
- The Element of Fire
- Passion
- Strength
- Fast action
- Career goals
- Lust
- Driving force
- Survival

Silver
- The Moon Goddess
- Astral energy
- Female energy
- Telepathy
- Clairvoyance
- Intuition
- Dreams

Copper
- Professional growth
- Business productivity
- Career manoeuvres
- Passion
- Money goals

Gold
- The Sun God
- Promote winning
- Male power
- Happiness

Yellow
- The Element of Air
- Intelligence
- The Sun
- Memory
- Imagination supported by logic
- Accelerating learning
- Clearing mental blocks

Signs from candle-burning

Not every magical practitioner takes heed of the manner in which spell-casting or ritual candles burn; there is often a great deal to be learnt from understanding a little bit more about how to interpret the way a candle burns.

It is worth remembering that some candles are simply poorly made and will burn badly no matter what you do with them. If the wick is the wrong size, for instance, the candle may be of no use for magical work. It is nice to make one's own candles, although there is quite an art to it and the novice may end up feeling rather frustrated, if the intention behind the candle is not quite right.

External factors can also play a huge part in how candles burn. The way the candle is placed in the holder, the temperature in the surrounding area, an open window causing a draught, and other such things can all make a difference. Equally, the candle can be affected by your own mood and really until you have learned how to meditate using a candle flame you need not worry too much to begin with. All that having been said, here are some of the things to watch for when burning candles.

The candle gives a clean, even burn This might be called a successful burn and suggests the spell will most likely achieve the right result. If a glass-encased candle burns and leaves no marks on the glass that is best. If a free-standing candle leaves little or no residue, this is by far the best result.

The flame flares, dips, gutters, repeatedly Check first for draughts and then decide intuitively whether there is a pattern to the flaring and guttering. If you are performing the spell with someone in mind, you may feel the recipient of your spell is trying to block your efforts. Sit quietly for a while until you feel you have grasped the significance of the pattern, which may be because the spell itself is not right for the time. In this case simply be prepared to try again another time.

A free-standing candle runs and melts a lot while burning This gives you an opportunity to observe the flow of wax for signs. Quickly melting wax shows there is a good deal of positivity available. If one side burns quicker than the other, a balance can sometimes be achieved by turning the candle round and it is useful to note how many times you do this, since this can indicate the number of adjustments the person may have to make to ensure success. Other people prefer to let nature take its course and to watch the wax run for signs, without interfering in its movements.

A free-standing candle burns down to a puddle of wax or sets in runs down the side of the candle When this happens, most workers will examine the shape of the wax for a sign. For instance, a heart-shaped wax puddle is a good sign if you are burning a red candle for a love spell. You may see something of importance there, for the shape of the run may suggest an outcome regarding the matter at hand. Wax puddles come in all kinds of shapes; most spell-workers look for symbols in the wax, or sometimes use numerology or other divination techniques similar to teacup reading, to discover meaning.

A glass-encased candle burns clean to begin with but 'dirty' with a great deal of smoke later This indicates that things will go well to begin with, but there are other conditions that have not yet revealed themselves and will need to be resolved. Someone may be working against the required outcome, so the correct timing and correspondences of further spells are crucial. Ensure you do spells to attract on a waxing moon (getting bigger in the sky) and spells to remove or bind on a waning moon (getting smaller).

A free-standing candle lets out a lot of smoke but burns clean at the end Difficult conditions need to be dealt with first of all but eventually conditions improve.

There is a dirty, black burn (especially one that deposits soot on a glass-encased candle) This means things are not going to go well – the spell may not work, the blessing may fail, the person is in deeper stress or trouble than you first thought. There is a great deal of negativity around. Sometimes it is good to change the focus of the candle and ask that it be used to burn off the negativity, which will enable you to get a handle on the situation.

The candle goes out before completely burning This can mean that the spell you are using is not the most appropriate one and you need to use stronger means than you first employed. It can also mean that someone is actively working against you. In this case it is wise to go back to the beginning and start your whole spell over again.

The candle tips over and flames up into a potential fire hazard Provided that you know you have placed the candles properly, this indicates there is danger about for you or the person you are casting for. You should clear your sacred space and cleanse it by whatever means you prefer. It is probably wise to wait a while before retrying the spell and remember to take a ritual bath (see page 75) before you do.

The candle burns too quickly Generally a fast burn is good, but an overly fast burn means that although the work will go well, its effect will not last long. Again, you might wait before retrying the spell, though sometimes a fast result is required. You should use your own judgement.

Disposal of candle wax

In European-American traditions, many people bury candle wax and other remains after a spell is cast. Burial toward the appropriate quarter of the compass is considered a thoughtful way to go about this. Some neo-pagans dispose of ritual or spell remains in a bonfire or fireplace.

HERBS

Most magical practices make use of herbs in various ways, usually in rituals and other magical workings. Often, they are used as incense, when they are crushed and powdered, or as oils. Their properties mean that they create a type of force field that intensifies the vibration needed. Additionally, when the practitioner calls upon the power of the gods and spirits, the herbs become even more effective.

Simply having particular herbs in your sacred space or having them about your person is sufficient to begin the process of enhancing the area or your personal vibration. You can use them in incense and dedicate them to the appropriate Elements and deities. Many of the herbs mentioned can be obtained from a good herbalist, though for those of you who are truly interested it would be worth while creating a small herb garden or growing them on your windowsill.

The uses of herbs

Protection
Such herbs guard against physical and psychic attacks, injury, accidents and such things as wicked spirits. They usually offer protection in a general sort of way.

Love
The vibration of these herbs is such that they can help you to meet new people, to overcome shyness and let others know that you are open to new relationships. They put out a particular vibration so that those who are interested will answer the call. The safest way to use them is to accept that several people may be attracted to you and you will then be able to make an informed choice.

Fidelity
Some herbs and plants can by tradition be used to ensure fidelity. You do have to have a firm belief that you have a right to another's devotion before imposing your will on them. Using a spell for fidelity amounts to a binding spell and you must make allowances for the person's own integrity. It should always be remembered that it is unwise, and sometimes unhelpful, to both parties to hold anyone in a relationship against their will.

Healing

Many herbs have healing properties, which can help from both a physical and a magical viewpoint. A practitioner working from both points of view can be of tremendous help in managing illness. However, always remember to advise anyone you work with in this way to seek qualified medical assistance. Never allow yourself to be drawn into being a substitute for medical help.

Health

Not only the smell of herbs and plants but also their vibration can help to prevent illness and restore good health. So, if you are prone to illness, carry health herbs with you and make sure they are always as fresh as possible.

Luck

Luck is the knack of being in the right place at the right time and being able to act on instinct. Luck herbs help you create your own good fortune. Once you have such a foundation, you can build upon it.

Money

It is sometimes easier to visualize the outcome of having money – that is, what you are going to spend the money on – than visualizing actual money coming to you. Certain herbs create an environment in which things can happen. They enable the creation of the means to fulfil your needs – perhaps a gift, a pay rise or some such thing.

The A–Z of Magical Plants

Aloe is feminine and ruled by the Moon. Its Element is Water. Its magical properties are protection, success and peace. Aloe has always been known for its healing qualities, for treating wounds and maintaining healthy skin. It helps to combat a variety of bacteria that commonly cause infections in skin wounds.

Amaranth (cockscomb) is feminine and ruled by Saturn. Its Element is Fire. When used magically, it is said to repair a broken heart, so therefore would be useful in certain love spells and rituals. Formerly it was reputed to bestow invisibility.

Angelica is a masculine plant ruled by Venus. Its Element is Fire. It is particularly useful when dealing with protection and exorcism; the root can be carried as an amulet with the dried leaves being burnt during exorcism rituals.

Anise is masculine and ruled by the Moon or Jupiter. Its Element is Air. Its magical properties are useful in protection and purification spells. It brings awareness and joy.

Apple is feminine and ruled by Venus. Its Element is Water. It is used most effectively in the making of magical wands, in love spells and good luck charms.

Ash is masculine and ruled by the Sun. Its Element is Water. Its uses are protective and it is often chosen as a material for making brooms for cleansing and wands for healing. If the leaves are put underneath a pillow, they will help to induce intuitive dreams. The leaves also bring luck and good fortune when carried in a pocket or bag worn around the neck.

Balm of Gilead is feminine and ruled by Saturn. Its Element is Water. The buds are carried to ease a broken heart and can be added to love and protection charms and spells.

Basil, one of the most masculine of plants, is ruled by Mars and has Fire as its Element. It is protective, good for love and is said to promote wealth and business success. It is also useful for healing relationships and for assuring genuineness in a partner.

Bay laurel is a masculine plant ruled by the Sun and the Element of Fire. It promotes wisdom and is also a protector, bringing to the fore the ability to develop psychic powers. It forces out negative energy.

Benzoin is a masculine plant that the Sun rules, along with the Element of Air. A good purifier and preservative, it is used widely in purification incenses.

Betony is masculine and is ruled by Jupiter and the Element of Fire. Its magical properties are protection and purification. It can be added to incense for this purpose or stuffed in a pillow to prevent nightmares.

Caraway is a masculine plant ruled by the planet of Mercury. Its Element is Air. Its magical properties are protection and passion. When added to love sachets and charms, it attracts a lover in the more physical aspect.

Carnation is masculine and is ruled by the Sun. Its Element is Fire. Traditionally, it was worn by witches for protection during times of persecution. It adds energy and power when used as an incense during a ritual.

Catnip is feminine and is ruled by Venus. Its Element is Water. Its magical properties are connected with cat magic, familiars, joy, friendship and love. As an incense it may be used to consecrate magical tools.

Camomile is masculine, and is ruled by the Sun or Venus. Its Element is Water. Its magical properties show that it is good as a meditation incense, for centring and creating an atmosphere of peace. Sprinkle it in your home for protection, healing and money. Plant camomile in your garden to be the guardian of the land, and you will have certain success. It is an excellent calming herb.

Celandine is masculine and is ruled by the Sun. Its Element is Fire. When worn as an amulet it helps the wearer to escape unfair imprisonment and entrapment. It alleviates depression.

Cinquefoil is masculine and is ruled by Jupiter. Its Element is Earth. Hang it around your doors and windows to protect you from evil. It is used in spells and charms for prosperity, purification and protection.

Cinnamon is masculine and is ruled by the Sun. Its Element is Fire. Its magical properties are used to help in spiritual quests, augmenting power, love, success, psychic work, healing and cleansing. It is used in incense for healing, clairvoyance and high spiritual vibrations; it is also reputed to be a male aphrodisiac. Use it in prosperity charms. It is an excellent aromatic and makes a good anointing oil for any magical working.

Clove is masculine and is ruled by the Sun. Its Element is Fire. Wear it in an amulet or charm to dispel negativity and bind those who speak ill of you. Cloves strung on a red thread can be worn as a protective charm. It helps with money matters, visions, cleansing and purification.

Clover is masculine and is ruled by Mercury; it is also associated with the Triple Goddess. Its Element is Air. Use it in rituals for beauty, youth, healing injuries, and helping alleviate mental difficulties. A four-leaved clover is said to enable one to see fairies and is considered a general good-luck charm.

Comfrey is a feminine plant and is ruled by Saturn. Its Element is Water. It is useful for travel, casting spells for money and healing. It also honours the Crone aspect of the Goddess.

Coriander is masculine and is ruled by Mars and the Element Fire. It is a protector of the home and is useful in the promotion of peace. It encourages longevity and is helpful in love spells.

Cowslip is feminine, ruled by Venus with its Element Water. Said to bring luck in love, it also induces contact with departed loved ones during dreams. A woman who washes her face with milk infused with cowslip will draw her beloved closer to her.

Cypress is masculine and is ruled by Saturn and its Element Earth. It is connected with death. Often used to consecrate ritual tools, cypress also has preservative qualities.

Daisy is feminine and is ruled by Venus and the Element Water. If you decorate your house with it on Midsummer's Eve, it will bring happiness into the home. Daisies are also worn at Midsummer for luck and blessings. Long ago, young maidens would weave daisy chains and wear them in their hair to attract their beloved.

Dandelion is masculine plant and is ruled by Jupiter and the Element Air. It is useful for divination and communication.

Dill is masculine and is ruled by Mercury. Its Element is Fire. It is useful in love charms. Dill may also be hung in children's rooms to protect them against evil spirits and bad dreams.

Dragon's blood is masculine, and is ruled by Mars with the Element Fire. A type of palm, it is widely included in love, protection and purification spells, usually in the form of a resin. It is carried for good luck; a piece of the plant kept under the bed is said to cure impotency. Dragon's blood increases the potency of other incense.

Elder is a feminine plant ruled by Venus and the Element Air. Its branches are widely used for magical wands and it is considered bad luck to burn elder wood. Leaves hung around the doors and windows are said to ward off evil.

Elecampane is a masculine plant ruled by Mercury and the Element Earth. It is a good aid in meditation and for requesting the presence of spirits.

Eucalyptus is feminine and is ruled by the Moon and the Element Air. It is used in healing rituals and in charms and amulets. If the leaves are put around a blue candle and burnt, this is good for increasing healing energies.

Eyebright is masculine and is ruled by the Sun. Its Element is Air. This plant is said to induce clairvoyant visions and dreams if you anoint the eyelids daily with an infusion of leaves.

Fennel is masculine and is ruled by Mercury. Its Element is Fire. Including the seeds in money charms is said to bring prosperity and ward off evil spirits. The plant itself is used for purification and protection.

Fern is feminine and is ruled by the planet Saturn and the Element Earth. This plant is a powerful protector and if grown near your home will ward off negativity.

Frankincense is a masculine herb under the rulership of the Sun and therefore the Element of Fire. A purifier of ritual spaces, it is probably the most powerful aid to meditation there is.

Gardenia is feminine and is ruled by the Moon with its Element Water. Used extensively in Moon incenses, it attracts good spirits to rituals and enhances the love vibration.

Garlic is a masculine herb ruled by the planet Mars and consequently the Element of Fire. It protects and is a useful healer and promoter of courage.

Ginger is a masculine herb ruled by Mars and Fire. It encourages power and success, especially in love and financial dealings. It is also a good base for spells because it enhances the vibration.

Ginseng is masculine, ruled by the Sun with the Element of Fire. It aids love and lust and is useful in enhancing beauty. It is also a good reliever of stress.

Hawthorn is masculine, ruled by Mars and the Element of Fire. It is used in protective sachets. It can enforce celibacy and chastity and is said to promote happiness in marriage or other relationships.

Hazel is masculine and ruled by the Sun and the Element of Air. It is a very good wood for magical wands and is the only wood that should be used for divining. It also promotes good luck, particularly when it is bound by red and gold thread.

Heartsease is feminine, ruled by Saturn and the Element of Water. It is actually a wild pansy and demonstrates its power by its name. If you can find any then it can be used with other herbs to ease the pain of a broken relationship.

Holly is masculine and is ruled by Mars and its Element of Fire. When planted around the home it protects against evil. Holly water is said to protect babies, and when thrown at wild animals it calms them down. The leaves and berries can be carried as an amulet by a man to heighten his masculinity and virility, enabling him to attract a lover.

Honeysuckle is feminine and is ruled by Jupiter and its Element Earth. Planted outside the home it brings good luck. It is also used in prosperity spells and love charms, and to heighten psychic ability.

Hops, a masculine plant ruled by Mars and the Element of Water, is best used in healing and for aiding sleep.

Hyssop is masculine. Its ruler is Jupiter and its Element of Fire. The plant was widely used during the Middle Ages for purification, cleansing and consecration rituals. Use it in purification baths, and for protective and banishing spells. Hyssop works best in the form of an essential oil in incense.

Ivy is a masculine plant, ruled by Saturn and its Element Water. It protects the houses it grows on from evil and harm. In the old traditions, ivy and holly were given to newly-weds as good-luck charms.

Jasmine is feminine and is ruled by Jupiter and the Element Earth. It attracts men through its scent and has been used throughout history by women for this purpose.

Juniper is a masculine plant, ruled by the Sun and its Element Fire. It gives protection against accidents, harm and theft. Once they have been dried and worn as a charm, the berries are used to attract lovers. Juniper also breaks hexes and curses.

Lavender is a masculine plant ruled by Mercury and the Element of Air. It is one of the most useful herbs and can be used for healing, promoting good wishes and sleep; it can also be used to attract men.

Lemon balm is feminine and is ruled by the Moon or Neptune. Its Element is Water. It is a strong aphrodisiac, promotes fertility but is also an anti-depressant that is especially useful at the end of a relationship.

Lemon verbena is feminine, ruled by Venus and the Element Air. It is used in love charms to promote youth, beauty and attractiveness to the opposite sex. Wear it around your neck or place it under a pillow to prevent bad dreams. It helps to heal wounds.

Lilac is a feminine plant that is ruled by the planet Venus. Its Element is Air. It is a good protector that also banishes evil and can be used for exorcism rituals.

Linden is feminine, ruled by Jupiter and its Element Water. It is said to be the tree of immortality and is associated with conjugal love or attraction and longevity. It is supposed to help in preventing intoxication.

Lovage is masculine, ruled by the Sun. Its Element is Water. The dried and powdered root should be added to cleansing and purification baths to release negativity. Carry it to attract love and the attention of the opposite sex. Also carry it when meeting new people.

Mandrake is a masculine plant ruled by Mercury and the Element Earth. It is very useful in incense for increasing the sex drive (both male and female) and is best used prior to the Full Moon.

Marigold is masculine and ruled by the Sun. Its Element is Fire. Prophecy, legal matters, the psyche, seeing magical creatures, love, divination dreams, business or legal affairs and renewing personal energy are all assisted by marigold. It is sometimes added to love sachets. It should be gathered at noon to be at its most powerful.

Marjoram is masculine and is ruled by Mercury with the Element Air. It protects against evil and aids love and healing; it is also helpful for those who are grieving.

Meadowsweet is feminine, its planet is Jupiter and it is ruled by Water. It is a sacred herb of the Druids and gives protection against evil influences; it also promotes love, balance and harmony. Place meadowsweet on your altar when making love charms and conducting love spells to increase their potency. It can be worn at Lammas to join with the Goddess.

Mint (spearmint and peppermint) is a masculine plant that is ruled by Mercury or Venus and has the Element Air. It promotes healing, the ability to gain money and is useful for successful travel. Known to aid digestion, it also calms the emotions.

Mugwort is a feminine plant that is ruled by Venus and the Element of Air. It is probably the most widely used herb by witches and promotes psychic ability and gives prophetic dreams. It is very good for astral projection.

Mullein is a masculine plant, ruled by Saturn and has the Element of Fire. This is used for courage and protection from wild animals and also from evil spirits. It is also used for cleansing and purifying ritual tools and altars and the cleansing of psychic places and sacred spaces before and after working. It guards against nightmares and can be substituted for graveyard dust.

Myrrh is a feminine plant that is ruled by the Moon or Jupiter and Water. It is purifying and protective and is especially useful when used with frankincense.

Myrtle is feminine, ruled by Venus, and its Element is Water. Myrtle was sacred to the Greek goddess Venus and has been used in love charms and spells throughout history. It should be grown indoors for good luck. Carry or wear myrtle leaves to attract love; charms made of the wood have special magical properties. Wear fresh myrtle leaves while making love charms, potions or during rituals for love and include it in them. Myrtle tea drunk every three days maintains youthfulness.

Nettle is a masculine plant ruled by Mars and its Element is Fire. It is a guard against danger and promotes courage.

Nutmeg is feminine, ruled by Jupiter, and its Element is Air. It helps to develop clairvoyance and psychic powers. When used with green candles it aids prosperity. It is also said to help teething.

Oak is masculine and is ruled by the Sun and the Element of Fire. It is often used by witches and used in power wands. It also protects against evil spirits and can also be used to promote a better sex life.

Orange is a feminine plant ruled by Jupiter and the Element of Water. It can be used as a love charm, while in the Orient it is used for good luck.

Orris root is a feminine plant, is ruled by Venus and has the Element of Water. The powder is used as a love-drawing herb and to increase sexual appeal. Used in charms, amulets, sachets, incenses and baths it will also protect you. Hung on a cord it can act as a pendulum.

Parsley is a masculine herb that is ruled by Mercury and Air. It wards off evil and is a useful aid to those who drink too much. Parsley may be used in purification baths and as a way to stop misfortune.

Patchouli is a feminine plant which is ruled by Saturn. Its Element is Earth. This plant is aphrodisiac and an attractant of lovers for either sex. It is sometimes used in fertility talismans and can be substituted for graveyard dust. Use it with green candles to ensure prosperity. Sprinkle it on money to spread your wealth.

Pennyroyal is a masculine plant ruled by Mars; its Element is Fire. It is used for protection, and, because it prevents weariness during long journeys, it is often carried on ships. Pennyroyal is also an insect deterrent. It should be avoided while pregnant.

Pepper (black) is a masculine plant which is ruled by Mars with its Element of Fire; it can be used in protective charms against the evil eye. Mixed with salt it dispels evil, which may be why it is used on food.

Pimpernel is a masculine plant which is ruled by Mercury and has the Element of Air. You should wear it to keep people from deceiving you. It wards off illness and stops accidents. The juice is used to purify and empower ritual weapons.

Pine is masculine and ruled by Mars; it has the Element of Air. It aids you to focus and if burnt it will help to cleanse the atmosphere where it is burnt. Its sawdust is often used as a base for incense, particularly in those associated with money.

Poppy is feminine, ruled by the Moon, and has the Element of Water. It is said that you can eat poppy seeds as a fertility charm; they can also be used in love sachets. Also carry the seeds or dried seed-pod as a prosperity charm.

Rose is a feminine plant that is ruled by Venus and the Element of Water. It is perhaps the most widely used plant in love and good-luck workings. Roses are also added to 'fast luck' mixtures designed to make things happen quickly. It is also a good calmer when situations become difficult.

Rosemary is a masculine plant that is ruled by the Sun and the Element of Fire. It improves memory and sleep; it is an excellent purifier. It should be used to cleanse your hands before performing magic or rituals. Hang it in doorways to prevent thieves entering.

Rowan is a masculine plant which is ruled by the Sun and the Element of Fire. Rowan wood is used for divining rods and wands; its leaves and bark are used in divination rituals. It is also used for protection, good luck and healing. When two twigs are tied together to form a cross it is a protective device.

Rue is masculine, ruled by the Sun and the Element of Fire. Protective when hung at a door, it can break hexes by sending the negativity back from whence it came. It is good for clarity of mind, clearing the mind of emotional clutter and purification of ritual spaces and tools.

Saffron is masculine, ruled by the Sun and the Element of Fire. It was used in rituals to honour the Goddess of the Moon, Ashtoreth. It dispels melancholy and restores sexual prowess in men. It is used to cleanse the hands in healing processes and is also used in prosperity incenses.

Sage is masculine, ruled by either Jupiter or Venus and the Element of Air. It promotes financial gain and good wishes; it is also a good healer and protector.

St John's Wort is a masculine plant that is ruled by the Sun and the Element of Fire. This protects against bad dreams and increases the willpower to do something difficult.

Sandalwood is feminine, ruled by the Moon, and its Element is Air. It has high spiritual vibrations so should be mixed with frankincense and burned at the time of the Full Moon. Anything visualized at this time is said to come true. It also clears negativity, so is good for purification, protection and healing workings.

Sunflower is masculine and is ruled by the Sun and the Element of Fire. It is extremely useful, for the seeds aid fertility while the plant allows you to discover the truth, if you sleep with it under your bed. It is said to guard the garden against marauders and pests.

Thyme is a feminine herb that is ruled by the planet Venus and the Element of Water. It is a good guardian against negative energy and an extremely good cleanser if combined with marjoram. It helps to develop psychic powers and is said to make women irresistible.

Valerian is feminine and is ruled by Venus and the Element of Water. One of the best sleep enhancers available, it also promotes love and rids your house of evil. It is said to protect against lightning.

Vanilla is feminine, ruled by Venus, and its Element is Water. The bean is used in a love charms, while the oil is worn as an aphrodisiac. Mix it with sugar to make love infusions.

Vervain is feminine and is ruled by Venus with the Element of Earth. Good for the ritual cleansing of sacred space, magical cleansing baths and purification incenses, it should be hung over the bed to prevent nightmares. Vervain is also excellent for use in prosperity charms and spells as it brings good luck and inspiration. It should be picked before sunrise. While it is said to control sexual urges (supposedly for seven years), it is also used in love and protection charms, presumably to ensure fidelity.

Violet is feminine, ruled by Venus, and its Element is Water. It brings changes in luck or fortune. Mix with lavender for a powerful love charm. A violet and lavender compress will help in eliminating headaches. The flowers are carried as a good-luck charm. The scent will soothe, clear the mind and relax the wearer.

Walnut is masculine, ruled by the Sun, and the Element is Fire. Carry the nut as a charm to promote fertility and strengthen the heart. It attracts lightning.

Willow is feminine and ruled by the Moon. The Element is Water. Willow wands can be used for healing and are at their strongest when used at the New Moon. Willow guards against evil and this is where the expression 'knock on wood' comes from.

Witch hazel is masculine, ruled by the Sun, with the Element of Fire. The wood is used to make divining rods. Witch hazel gives protection and promotes chastity, healing the heart. It cools all the passions.

Wormwood is masculine, ruled by Mars, with the Element of Air. Wormwood is poisonous but is sometimes burned in smudge sticks to gain protection from wandering spirits. It is said that it enables the dead to be released from this plane so they may find peace. It is also used in divinatory and clairvoyance incenses, initiation rites and tests of courage. Mixed with sandalwood, it summons spirits.

Yarrow is feminine and ruled by Venus. Its Element is Water. There is evidence that yarrow was often a component in incense used for incantations. It is a powerful incense additive for divination and love spells, too. It exorcises evil, dispelling negativity, yet also enhances psychic ability and divination. Yarrow tea drunk prior to divination will enhance powers of perception; a touch of peppermint enhances the action of this brew and always helps it to work better. The plant is also used in courage, love and marriage charms.

Yucca is masculine, and ruled by Mars. Its Element is Fire. Yucca is said to help with shape-shifting. If a strand of a leaf is tied around one's head and then an animal is visualized the wearer becomes (takes on the qualities of) that animal. Yucca is used to purify the body before performing magic. To get rid of illness, bathe at least twice using suds from the boiled plant juices. A cross formed from yucca leaves is said to protect the hearth, the centre of the home.

Making a Herb Bundle

The first thing to remember when you are making your herb bundle is that, as with any spiritual intent, be sure to wash and cleanse yourself – deliberately getting rid of any negative energy in the process – before you begin. There are also a few other guidelines you'll need to follow.

- Before picking the plant matter, honour the plant and ask its permission to take a branch or stem for your spiritual intent. Respect the plant and let it continue to give of its life.
- When picking stems, make sure they are long enough to be bound together.
- Use any of the herbs mentioned above or use pine or cypress, if your location allows. You do not have to use plants and herbs that are in your immediate vicinity – though, if you have grown the plants yourself, this will give you tremendous satisfaction.
- If you want to, add essential oils, but use them sparingly and try to choose one that will enhance the purpose of, or add an extra quality to, your bundle.

YOU WILL NEED
Selection of leaves and stems
Elastic band
Thick cotton twine
Small bowl

METHOD
Arrange a small handful of leaves and stems fairly symmetrically into a bundle – don't use too many.

Put the stems in the elastic band to keep the pieces together while you tie the bundle, removing it when you have finished.

Take a long piece of thick cotton twine and place the bundle top (the thicker end) in the middle of it.

Using the two ends of the twine, bind the bundle together tightly in a criss-cross fashion, starting at the top and finishing at the bottom part of the stems. (Take your time over this – the more secure you make the bundle, the better it will burn. Some leaves or twigs may protrude, so you need a receptacle to catch falling ashes.)

Bind the end of your bundle securely with the twine and perhaps make a dedication to your purpose.

You will now have a cone-shaped bundle. Let it dry out thoroughly before burning it, because it won't burn properly if it is at all damp.

To use the herb bundle, light the thicker top end and then blow out the flame out so it smoulders. Some bits may drop out of the bundle so remember to have a bowl or receptacle handy to catch them.

Herb bundles are moved to where the fragrant smoke is needed. In rituals, you would use the cardinal points. Walk around slowly, wafting the smoke into the corners of the room as you do so. (You may have to keep blowing on the lit end to keep it burning.) As you blow, remember that you are using the principle of Air. You can also direct the smoke with either of your hands, the small branch of a plant, or even a special crystal or stone. Amber can also be used – especially appropriate as it is a resin from a plant. This action should get rid of any negative vibrations at the same time as energizing the protective frequencies.

If you want to cleanse the energy of a friend (or yourself), waft the smoke all around the body, starting at the head and gradually moving down to the feet. Move in a clockwise direction because this creates positivity. You can direct the smoke with your hand or a feather or whatever feels good for you. A seashell is a good idea since it represents the Goddess. You can also chant or sing at this time. Whatever you do, do it with a pure mind and spirit. When you have finished, keep the bundle safe until it has extinguished itself and then open a window to clear the space.

Decorative bundles
If you don't intend to burn the bundle then there are many other possibilities open to you. Bundles can be bound with colour, feeling and meaning. Oils will add energy and aroma. You can use spices, fruits, fragrant wood, minerals, crystals, resins or flowers like rose, marigold or lavender. Depending on how you plan to display the bundle, you can use pretty much anything that has meaning and fragrance.

INCENSE

As well as making use of herbs as plants, decorations and for healing, their most important use in magic was – and still is – in incense. Incense symbolizes the Element Air and the spiritual realms and has been part of ritual use by magical workers and priests alike for thousands of years. Granular incense, with its basis of resins and gums, is nowadays usually preferred for magical workings or ritual worship. It has a magic all of its own. For this reason a good incense burner will be one of your most important tools. You should choose this carefully, and not just for its aesthetic sense, because it is vital that the incense is allowed to burn properly.

Since time immemorial, people have burned sweet-smelling woods, herbs and resins to perfume, cleanse and clarify the atmosphere in which they exist. During outdoor rituals special woods and herbs with magical qualities would be thrown onto bonfires or into altar cauldrons. In the home, open-hearth fires could be used to give off perfumed smoke which sweetened or freshened the air. The word 'perfume' means 'through smoke'.

Initially, resins and gums were used most successfully, so in areas where resinous trees grew, incenses were used to honour the gods. Egypt became especially renowned for its high standard of blending and the use of ritual incense. There was a particular class of incense – which is still available today – called Kyphi or Khyphi. It required magical techniques and the finest ingredients for its manufacture.

Kyphi Incense
1 part myrrh resin
1 part frankincense resin
1 part gum arabic
1 part Balm of Gilead buds
1 part cassia or cinnamon
Few drops of lotus oil
Few drops of musk oil

Nowadays incense is most often encountered in the form of joss sticks, which were introduced to the West in the 1960s by travellers to India who brought them back with them. For short rituals these work very well, though they are not to everyone's taste. Dhoop, or incense cones, as they are known, are another way of using the same material.

The best method of using incense is to burn the granular type on a charcoal disc. By this method the charcoal disc is lit and placed in a fireproof receptacle. The incense is then piled onto the concave surface and allowed to do its work. After use, the charcoal discs remain very hot. You should dispose of them very carefully, dousing them with water and ensuring they are no longer 'alive' and thus potentially harmful. You might like to bury what remains of the incense as an offering to the earth.

Making and using incenses

Many of the herbs already discussed are suitable for incense, if you wish to make your own. You should choose your correspondences carefully, according to your spell or ritual, and may like to make incense in tune with the cycles of life and planetary correspondences. You will soon find out through experimentation what works for you. You can also use essential oils as part of your incense-making, if you so wish.

The use of incense in magical workings can be quite a personal act of worship; the various blends can sometimes either appeal to your senses or smell absolutely foul, often depending on your mood. For this reason, a number of blends from numerous sources are given here. Experiment until you settle on your own particular favourites and then work from there.

There does need to be some clarification of the lists of ingredients, however. A 'part' indicates one measure or a proportion, which may be a teaspoon, a cup and so forth. Fractions indicate portions of a part. Personal experience shows that making small quantities is best as the incense then stays fresher and is often more cost-effective. If you plan on making quantities of several types of incense, collect a number of individual portion jars in which jams and honeys are packed. Such an amount is ideal for your immediate use.

Unless otherwise specified, use dried herbs, flowers, roots and resins, since these are often both easier to get hold of than fresh and are packed in suitable quantities and compositions for incense-making. The more unusual herbs, oils and resins can usually be obtained from any good herbalist, and there are now also several suppliers who can deliver by mail order and will often blend their own mixtures.

Initial purchase of the various ingredients is quite expensive, so if you work with other people you may wish to share the cost in some way. Start off with the first ingredient, grind it small and then add each subsequent ingredient in small quantities until it smells and feels right to you.

Incense Preparation

This is an accepted way of making incense, but you do need to be patient. The art of blending is highly skilled and your own experiments will show you the best methods for you. If you know your correspondences, you can call on the various deities to help you in your task, or just simply bear in mind the ultimate purpose of your incense. Most oils and binders such as the gums are added last.

YOU WILL NEED
Pestle and mortar
(Your pestle and mortar can be of any material, though one that does not pick up the perfumes of the ingredients is obviously best. If you do not have a pestle and mortar, a chopping board and rolling pin will suffice, though it is messier this way.)
Set of measuring spoons
Large bowl in which to blend your mixture thoroughly
Your chosen herbs, resins, oils etc.
Small containers with lids
Labels
Charcoal blocks for burning the incense

METHOD
Make sure that you grind each quantity of the herbs and resins as small as possible.

When each ingredient is ground, place it in your large bowl, reserving a small quantity in the right proportions of each ingredient with which to do a test run.

Mix in each ingredient thoroughly as you add it to the bowl. Mixing by hand is probably most successful, since this allows you to introduce your own personal vibration. You could also use a wand of sacred wood reserved specifically for the purpose if you wish.

As you mix, say:

May this herb [resin/oil] enhance the power
of this offering for the spirits of Air

Add any oil last and make sure that this is thoroughly mixed in and not left in one place in the mixture.

47

When all ingredients are combined, spend some time
thinking about your purpose and gently mixing and
remixing your incense.

Remember that if you are making incense for a particular
purpose, the herbs and resins used should correspond to that
purpose, therefore your incense may not necessarily smell
as pleasant as you would like.

If wished, ask for a blessing or consecration for the
incense, as follows:

May this the work of my two hands
Be blessed for the purpose of [state purpose]

Now test your sample by lighting a charcoal block, placing the
incense on it then burning it carefully in a safe place.

Your incense is now ready, though it is best not to use it for at least 24
hours to enable the perfumes and qualities to blend properly. Many
incenses blend, change and strengthen when stored correctly and incense
often improves with keeping, so your sample may not smell the same
as your stored incense. If it is to your liking and you feel it is suitable
for your purpose, fill the containers, secure them tightly and label them
clearly. They should be stored in a cool, dark place.

Incense Blends

Banishing, Exorcism and Purification

All the following incenses work on the principle that certain energies
need to be banished in order for the practitioner to work effectively. The
creation of peace, purification of the area and, of course, exorcism of
unwanted spirits all come under this heading. Do think very carefully
about what you wish to achieve before deciding which incense is right
for your purpose. Suggestions are given here or the purpose is clearly
indicated in the title.

It is always possible to make substitutions in the ingredients. They
can all be mixed and matched ad infinitum, though you may have to
experiment with the quantities until the incense 'feels' right (or until it
smells right). Use your intuition to find the right blend for your purpose.

Banishing and Exorcism

Banishing Incense
1 *part bay leaves*
2 *parts cinnamon*
1 *part rose petals*
2 *parts myrrh resin*
pinch of salt

Clearing Incense
1 *part frankincense resin*
1 *part copal resin*
1 *part myrrh resin*
½ *part sandalwood*

Burn this with the windows open.

Exorcism Incense
3 *parts frankincense resin*
1 *part rosemary*
1 *part bay leaves*
1 *part avens*
1 *part mugwort*
1 *part St John's Wort*
1 *part angelica*
1 *part basil*

Burn this incense with the windows open to drive out very heavy spiritual negativity from your surroundings.

Ending Negativity Incense
1 *part marjoram*
1 *part thyme*
½ *part oregano*
¼ *part bay leaves*
¼ *part cloves*

Jinx-removing Incense
2 *parts clove*
1 *part deerstongue*
Few drops of rose geranium oil

This incense can be used when you think someone is against you.

Uncrossing Incense
2 *parts lavender*
1 *part rose*
2 *parts bay*
1 *part verbena*

Use this incense when you feel you or your home has been 'cursed' or you are under attack.

Purification

Purification Incense 1
2 *parts sandalwood*
1 *part cinnamon*
2 *parts bay*
1 *part vervain*
pinch of salt

Burn this incense with the windows open to clear a disturbed home after an argument, for instance.

Purification Incense 2
2 *parts sandalwood*
1 *part cinnamon*

Leave the windows open to clear an atmosphere quickly.

Purification Incense 3
3 parts frankincense resin
2 parts dragon's blood resin
1 part myrrh resin
1 part sandalwood
1 part wood betony
½ part dill seed
Few drops of rose geranium oil

This is good for clearing your new home of old energies.

Domestic Tranquility Incense
¾ part sage
¼ part rue
½ part ground ivy

Few drops of bayberry oil
¼ part bayberry
1¼ parts linden

Hearth and Home Incense
2 parts dragon's blood resin
½ part juniper
½ part sassafrass
½ part orange flowers
2 parts myrrh resin
½ part rose petals

This incense should be burnt when you wish to create a safe, warm, loving home.

Protection

There are many ways of protecting both yourself and your own space by the use of incense. If you simply wish to protect against the intrusion of negative energies, it is probably best to use those incenses that are based mainly on the resinous substances. This is for two reasons. First, most resins are relatively slow-burning, high-vibrational energy substances, so their effect is long-lasting; secondly, you have more opportunity when grinding them to introduce specific intents into the incense. Perhaps, for instance, you might wish to protect yourself against the jealousy of a former lover or against financial loss. Using substances that have a high vibration helps to build a 'wall' of protection, which means that neither the bad thought nor the subtle energies activated on a more spiritual level can harm you.

Some of the incenses below are specifically to protect against not just negativity on a purely physical plane, but also malign energy deliberately directed at you and your loved ones. Incense such as the ones for psychic protection will give you the security you need to know that you can combat such gross intrusion.

Other incenses mean that you can react quickly to outside influences should you need to do so. There are many alternatives in this, as in other sections, so that you can decide for yourself which ones work best for you. A lot will depend on what is local to you, and so far as protection incenses are concerned, the sensitivities can change depending on the environment surrounding the individual. Where the incense is for a specific purpose, that information is given. Once again, it is always possible when making these incenses to substitute the ingredients. They can all be mixed and matched ad infinitum, though you may have to experiment with the quantities until they 'feel' right (or until they smell right) to you.

Peace and Protection Incense
4 parts lavender
3 parts thyme
2 parts vervain
3 parts basil
1 part frankincense resin
Pinch of rue
Pinch of benzoin resin
Few drops of bergamot oil
Few drops of jasmine oil

This can be used in both peace and protection spells and rituals.

Protection Incense 1
½ part bay leaves
½ part cloves
¾ part oregano
¾ part sandalwood

Protection Incense 2
4 parts verbena
1 part galangal root (ground)
1 part peppermint
1 part cinnamon
½ part rue

Protection Incense 3
¼ part basil
½ part cinnamon
½ part rosemary
1½ parts thyme
½ part sage
½ part star anise

Total Protection Incense
2 parts frankincense resin
1 part dragon's blood resin
½ part wood betony

This incense creates quite a high vibration and protects on all levels of existence.

Iron Protection Incense
¼ part iron filings
1 part galangal root (powdered)
Few drops of citronella oil

This incense uses the ancient idea that iron will change a negative vibration.

New Orleans Protection Incense
2 parts myrrh resin
½ part bay leaves
1 part cloves
1 part cinnamon

This is an incense often used in Hoodoo work.

Sandalwood Protection Incense
3 parts sandalwood
2 parts juniper
1 part vetivert

Pennyroyal Protection Incense
2 parts verbena or vetivert

1 part galangal
1 part pennyroyal
¼ part rue
½ part cinnamon

Rosemary Protection Incense
2 parts rosemary
½ part orris root (ground)
1 part basil
1 part frankincense resin

10 Herb Protection Incense
2 parts frankincense resin
2 parts myrrh resin
1 part juniper berries
½ part rosemary
¼ part avens
¼ part mugwort
¼ part yarrow
¼ part St John's Wort
½ part angelica
1 part basil

5 Resins Protection Incense
2 parts frankincense resin
1 part copal resin
1 part myrrh resin
½ part dragon's blood resin
½ part gum arabic

Home Protection Incense
½ part frankincense resin
¾ part sage
½ part basil
½ part mistletoe
¼ part garlic (mix of dried and
    ground)
¾ part rosemary
¼ part rue
1 part sandalwood

½ part myrrh resin
½ part orris root
½ part yarrow

Note: The next two incenses can
be used if you wish to protect
your surroundings against theft
and burglary.

Prevent Theft Incense
1 part ground ivy
½ part juniper
1½ parts rosemary

Stop Theft Incense
½ part dogwood
¼ part caraway
½ part rosemary
¼ part tarragon
1 part willow
Few drops honeysuckle oil

Note: The next four incenses
deal specifically with protection
on a psychic level, while the two
following deal with the effects of
an unwanted spiritual visitation.
They could be considered to
belong to the banishing and
exorcism categories.

Psychic Protection Incense 1
½ part elder
1 part cinquefoil
½ part bay leaves
⅛ part valerian

Psychic Protection Incense 2
¼ part broom
½ part agrimony

½ part basil
¼ part cranesbill
1 part vetivert
½ part oregano

Psychic Protection Incense 3
¼ part frankincense resin
½ part oregano
¼ part lovage
½ part cloves
¼ part ginger root (ground)
½ part sandalwood
¼ part star anise

Psychic Protection Incense 4
½ part benzoin resin
¼ part dragon's blood resin
½ part frankincense resin
¼ part camphor gum
½ part cassia
¼ part patchouli
2 parts sandalwood

Each ingredient in this incense is a resin.

Note: These next two incenses help to keep your home clear of spirit interference unless you have specifically asked for spirit to be present.

Spirits Depart Incense
2 parts fennel seed
2 parts dill seed
½ part rue

Spirit Portal Incense
½ part cinnamon
½ part lavender

pinch of wormwood
Note: The next five protection incenses all have as their main ingredients resins, particularly frankincense. If you dislike the perfume of frankincense, experiment with the proportions of your other resins.

Frankincense Protection Incense 1
4 parts frankincense resin
3 parts myrrh resin
2 parts juniper berries
1 part rosemary
½ part avens
½ part mugwort
½ part yarrow
½ part St. John's Wort
½ part angelica
½ part basil

This incense is so all-enveloping that it will protect against almost everything.

Frankincense Protection Incense 2
2 parts frankincense resin
1 part dragon's blood powder or
   resin
½ part betony

This incense is particularly potent when attempting to visualize the source of your problem.

Frankincense Protection Incense 3
2 parts frankincense resin
1 part sandalwood
½ part rosemary

Frankincense Protection Incense 4
1 part frankincense resin
1 part myrrh resin
½ part clove

Frankincense Protection Incense 5
2 parts frankincense resin
1 part copal resin
1 part dragon's blood powder or resin

Lust, Love and Relationships

The idea of trying to influence someone else directly goes against the ethics of many practitioners and magicians. One must be very careful because incense prepared with the intention of trying to make someone do that which they do not want to, or which goes against their natural inclination, can possibly misfire and cause the originator of such a spell a good deal of difficulty.

Love incense really should only be used with the intent that the occurrence will only be in accordance with the Greater Good, whether it be the beginning or the ending. That is, that you are helping something to happen, not forcing it. Apart from that, many of these incenses have a beautiful perfume and can help to create a loving, supportive atmosphere.

It is always possible when preparing incense to make substitutions in the ingredients. They can all be mixed and matched ad infinitum, though you may have to experiment with the quantities until they 'feel' right (or until they smell right).

There are many different aspects to relationships. In this section the individual titles of each recipe are self-explanatory.

Loving Friends Incense
½ part acacia
1 part rosemary
¼ part elder
½ part frankincense resin
1 part dogwood

Attract a Lover Incense
1 part lovage
½ part orris root (ground)
1 part lemon verbena
¼ part patchouli
Few drops of lemon verbena oil

Attract Love Incense
½ part cloves
1 part rose
¼ part saw palmetto
½ part juniper
Few drops of musk oil
Few drops of rose oil
½ part red sandalwood

Draw and Strengthen Love Incense
2 parts sandalwood
½ part basil
½ part bergamot

Few drops of rose oil
Few drops of lavender oil

Love Incense 1
1 part orris root (ground)
Few drops musk oil
1 part sandalwood
1 part violet
Few drops of gardenia oil

Love Incense 2
2 parts dragon's blood resin
1 part orris root (ground)
½ part cinnamon
½ part rose petals
Few drops of musk oil
Few drops of patchouli oil

Love Incense 3
1 part patchouli
Few drops of musk oil
Few drops of civet oil
Few drops of ambergris oil

This incense makes the opposite sex more aware of you.

Love Incense 4
1 part violets
1 part rose petals
½ part olive leaves

Love Incense 5
2 parts sandalwood
2 parts benzoin resin
1 part rosebuds
Few drops of patchouli oil
Few drops of rose oil

Love Incense 6
2 parts sandalwood
½ part basil
½ part bergamot
Few drops of rose oil
Few drops of lavender oil

Burn this incense to attract love, to strengthen the love you have and also to expand your ability to give and receive love.

Increase Love Incense
½ part benzoin
¼ part jasmine
1 part rose
¼ part patchouli
½ part musk root
½ part sandalwood
Few drops of musk oil
Few drops of civet oil
Few drops of rose oil
Few drops of jasmine oil

This incense can be used in love rituals when you wish to strengthen the bonds between you.

Note: The next three incenses are all thought to have an effect on the libido.

Fiery Passion Incense
¾ part yohimbe
½ part cinnamon
¼ part ginger root
2½ parts damiana
Few drops of ambergris oil

Passion Incense
½ part cranesbill
1¼ parts cascara
½ part savory
Few drops of civet oil
½ part musk root

Physical Love Incense
¾ part damiana
½ part yohimbe
½ part musk root
¾ part cascara
Few drops of bergamot oil
Few drops of ambergris oil

Fidelity Incense
¼ part basil
¼ part dragon's blood resin
1 part red sandalwood
½ part rosemary
1 part dogwood
Few drops of honeysuckle oil

Marital Bliss Incense
1 part vanilla bean (ground)
2 parts wintergreen
1 part khus khus
1 part narcissus
Few drops of wintergreen oil

Burn this incense at night, just before you go to bed.

Note: The following five incenses should be used carefully because it is not wise to try to influence someone against their will. Your choice of words when performing the ritual is important.

Stay at Home Incense
½ part clove
½ part allspice
½ part deerstongue
1 part mullein
1 part sage

Divorce Incense
½ part frankincense resin
½ part rue
½ part allspice
¼ part marjoram
¾ part pennyroyal
½ part yarrow
⅛ part camphor resin
½ part sandalwood

End an Affair Incense
¼ part menthol
1½ parts willow
1½ parts lavender

Love Breaker Incense
½ part vetivert
1 part patchouli
1 part lemongrass
½ part mullein

This incense can be used to aid the smooth break-up of a relationship.

Release and Ending Incense
½ part bay
½ part lemon balm
¼ part yarrow
½ part pennyroyal
1 part willow
Few drops of lemon balm oil
Few drops of peppermint oil

Business, Money, Prosperity and Success

After love incense, incense that can be used to bring about success in business affairs and finance are the ones that intrigue people most. On the quiet, many business people who use incense would concede that they have received assistance, but they would hate to admit it publicly. These incenses are especially appropriate for those who value secrecy, because they can be used without fuss to create circumstances where the desired effect becomes inevitable.

Using these incenses might be considered by some to be employing thaumaturgy – magic that is designed to have an effect specifically on the mundane world. Wherever possible, keep your intent as altruistic and as clearly in mind as you can when using incense. The 'higher' the intent, the more likely it is to happen because it can be said to be in accord with the Greater Good. It is suggested that any prosperity, money or success you receive as a consequence is tithed; that is, a portion is dedicated to good causes – in old-style belief, 10 per cent.

It is always possible when preparing incense to make substitutions in the ingredients. They can all be mixed and matched ad infinitum, though you may have to experiment with the quantities until they 'feel' right (or until they smell right).

Business

These first ten incenses are burnt when you wish to increase your personal portfolio and business acumen. Burning the confidence incenses, for instance, will help you to gain confidence, but only if you have something to build on in the first place.

Business Incense
2 parts benzoin resin
1 part cinnamon
1 part basil

Confidence Incense 1
1 part rosemary
¼ part garlic
½ part camomile
1 part musk root

Confidence Incense 2
1 part St John's Wort
1 part thyme

½ part oak
¼ part sweet woodruff

Recognition Incense
2 parts benzoin resin
1 part rue
1 part sandalwood

This incense can be used when you feel your efforts should be recognized and rewarded.

Note: These next three incenses should be used when you require

57

a little extra 'oomph' to carry you along a chosen path.

Determination Incense 1
½ part althea
½ part camomile
1 part thyme
¼ part garlic

Determination Incense 2
1 part rosemary
1 part willow
1 part musk root
Few drops of musk oil

Determination Incense 3
½ part allspice
1¼ parts St John's Wort
½ part southernwood
¾ part willow

Note: These following two incenses can be used to encourage the flow of money towards you.

Financial Gain Incense 1
1 part lovage
1 part bay
¼ part cinnamon
½ part meadowsweet

Financial Gain Incense 2
½ part star anise
¼ part poppy seed
½ part mistletoe
½ part juniper
1 part cherry

Financial Increase Incense
¼ part cucumber
¾ part allspice

1 part sunflower
¼ part saw palmetto
½ part marigold

This incense can be used when you are deliberately wishing to increase what you already have; that is, make a profit, rather than simply gain money.

Note: These following two incenses may be used when additional information or insight is needed either in specific circumstances or on a day-to-day basis. They are good incenses to burn in a training situation.

Gain Knowledge and Wisdom Incense 1
¼ part angelica
¼ part vervain
1 part sage
½ part Solomon's Seal

Knowledge and Wisdom Incense 2
1 part Solomon's Seal
¼ part benzoin resin
½ part vervain
½ part cloves
½ part bay

Money Incense 1
1 part basil
1 part cinquefoil
½ part hyssop
½ part galangal

Money Incense 2
1¼ parts lavender

¼ part camomile
¼ part comfrey
1 part red clover
¼ part acacia

More Money Incense
¾ part cinnamon
½ part dragon's blood resin
1¼ parts cascara

Note: These next five incenses are good for accruing more than your immediate needs. The last two enable you to call in, and give, favours when necessary.

Prosperity Incense
1 part frankincense resin
½ part cinnamon
¼ part nutmeg
½ part balm

Wealth Incense
1 part nutmeg
½ – 1 part pepperwort
1 pinch saffron

Increased Wealth Incense
2 parts frankincense resin
1 part cinnamon
1 part nutmeg
½ part clove
½ part ginger
½ part mace

Riches and Favours Incense 1
2 parts benzoin resin
½ part clove
½ part pepperwort

Riches and Favours Incense 2
2 parts benzoin resin
1 part wood aloe
½ part peppermint
½ part clove

Note: These next three incenses are used to pull success towards you, whatever you may perceive that to be.

Success Incense 1
½ part basil
½ part bay
1 part cedar
½ part oak

Success Incense 2
¼ part mistletoe
½ part marigold
½ part sunflower
¼ part onion
1 part sandalwood

Success Incense 3
¼ part frankincense resin
½ part sweet woodruff
1½ parts vetivert
¼ part angelica
1 part sandalwood

Note: This following incense can be used when you wish to build on success you have already had.

Greater Success Incense
1½ parts sandalwood
½ part sarsaparilla
½ part motherwort
½ part quassia
Few drops of jasmine oil

Luck

These next four incenses are all designed to bring good fortune. Your intent is very important when you use a first-rate luck incense. The incenses open the way to winning, rather than actually winning for you.

Good Luck in Life Incense
½ part musk root
1½ part rose
½ parts red clover
½ part galangal root
Few drops of rose oil

Good Luck Incense
½ part dragon's blood resin
½ part mistletoe
1 part cascara
1 part linden

Improve Luck Incense
1 part rosemary
½ part dragon's blood resin
½ part musk root
½ part sandalwood
Few drops of rose oil
Few drops of musk oil

Games of Chance Incense
½ part dragon's blood resin
2 parts gum mastic resin
1 part frankincense resin

This incense could be used, for example, when you wish to try your luck and place a bet.

Physical and Emotional Health and Healing

Any incense used for the purpose of health and healing should only be used as an adjunct to other methods. If you are prepared to use incense in this way, you will probably have an awareness of alternative healing methods anyway, but they cannot – and should never – be used as substitutes for proper medical advice.

Many of the herbs given here are those which have been used for centuries to alleviate certain conditions, but bearing in mind modern laws and thought, you must make your own decisions as to their effective use. Seek the help of your herbalist or medical practitioner as to the nature of the ingredients and what form they should take (root, powder, and so forth).

It is always possible when preparing incense to make substitutions in the ingredients. They can all be mixed and matched ad infinitum, though you may have to experiment with the quantities until they 'feel' right (or until they smell right).

Physical Health

Cold-healing Incense
1¼ *parts pine*
½ *part cedar*
⅛ *part camphor*
⅛ *part menthol*
½ *part spruce*
Few drops of pine oil

Resins have always had their part to play in incense. This particular incense will help ease the symptoms of a cold – you can see from its ingredients it is as much medicinal as magical.

Healing Incense 1
2 *parts myrrh resin*
1 *part cinnamon*
1 *pinch saffron*

Healing Incense 2
1 *part rose*
1 *part eucalyptus*
1 *part pine*
1 *pinch saffron*

Healing Incense 3
1 *part rosemary*
1 *part juniper*

When used in oil form – that is, on a tissue placed on a radiator or in a burner – this incense is easily used in a hospital environment.

Regain Health Incense
3 *parts myrrh resin*
2 *parts nutmeg*
1 *part cedar*
1 *part clove*
½ *part balm*
½ *part poppy seeds*
Few drops of pine oil
Few drops of sweet almond oil

This incense acts as a good 'pick-me-up'.

Emotional Health
All of these incenses help to alter the state of mind and increase the ability to think positively.

Courage Incense
2 *parts dragon's blood powder*
   or resin
1 *part frankincense resin*
1 *part rose geranium*
¼ *part tonka beans*
Few drops of musk oil

Ease Emotional Pain Incense
3 *parts bay*
¾ *part allspice*
¼ *part dragon's blood powder*
¾ *part frankincense resin or*
gum arabic

End Negativity and Give Hope Incense 1
1 part thyme
½ part rue
½ part sweet woodruff
½ part cloves

End Negativity and Give Hope Incense 2
1 part dittany
½ part camomile
¼ part patchouli

Happiness Incense 1
½ part myrrh resin
¼ part marjoram
1 part dittany
¾ part sandalwood
¾ part oregano
Few drops of spearmint oil

Happiness Incense 2
1 part oregano
1 part rosemary
1 part marigold

'Poor Me' Incense
½ part cloves
¼ part juniper
2 parts willow
⅛ part menthol
Few drops of eucalyptus oil
Few drops of wintergreen oil

This incense can be used for when you feel the whole world is against you.

Tranquility Incense
1 part sage
1½ parts rose
¼ part benzoin resin
½ part meadowsweet
Few drops of rose oil

This incense induces a sense of tranquility which allows you to rebalance and recharge your batteries.

Note: These next two incenses give strength and integrity in a chosen task.

Strength Incense 1
½ part dragon's blood powder or resin
½ part musk root
1½ parts vetivert
½ part cinquefoil
Few drops of musk oil
Few drops of Ambergris oil

Strength Incense 2
½ part cinnamon
¼ part dragon's blood powder or resin
¼ part frankincense resin
½ part musk root
¼ part patchouli
1 part vetivert
¼ part yarrow
Few drops of musk oil

Study Incense
2 parts gum mastic
1 part rosemary

Burn this incense to strengthen the conscious mind for study, to develop concentration and to improve your memory.

Psychic Powers, Divination and Prophetic Dreams
Remembering that the use of mind-altering substances should be very carefully considered, this section sets about indicating substances that alter your sensitive vibrational rate. Each one of us consists of at least a physical body, an astral body and a spiritual aspect. These subtle energies can be successfully adjusted to connect us with other subtle vibrations – it is a little like logging on to a computer and connecting with a particular programme.

The incenses below help us to do this and enable us to work without interference from other less manageable energies. They put us in touch with those inner powers that we use to penetrate other dimensions and help us to develop them without disquiet. Their specific purpose is, by and large, stated in the name of the incense.

It is always possible when preparing incense to make substitutions in the ingredients. They can all be mixed and matched ad infinitum, though you may have to experiment with the quantities until they 'feel' right (or until they smell right).

Divination
The following six incenses can be used as part of divinatory rituals.

Divination Incense 1
1 part St John's Wort
¾ part wormwood
¾ part bay
½ part frankincense resin

Divination Incense 2
¾ part cinquefoil
⅛ part valerian
½ part deerstongue
½ part frankincense resin
1 part sandalwood

Divination Incense 3
½ part cinnamon
½ part chickweed
1 part thyme
1 part sandalwood

Divination Incense 4
1 part yarrow
1 part St John's Wort
¼ part frankincense resin
½ part bay

Divination Incense 5
1 part lavender
1 part rose
½ part star anise
½ part sandalwood

Divination Incense 6
2 parts sandalwood
1 part orange peel
½ part mace
½ part cinnamon

Psychic Powers

These next four incenses are particularly good for enhancing the psychic powers during magical rituals.

Psychic Power Incense
1 part frankincense resin
¼ part bistort

Psychic Incense 1
2 parts sandalwood
1 part gum arabic

Psychic Incense 2
2 parts sandalwood
1 part gum acacia (or arabic)

Psychic Incense 3
1 part frankincense resin
1 part sandalwood
1 part cinnamon
1 part nutmeg
Few drops of orange oil
Few drops of clove oil

Past Lives

These next two incenses can be used when you wish to find out about past lives.

Recall Past Lives Incense
1½ parts sandalwood
½ part water lily
½ part holly
½ part frankincense resin
Few drops of lilac oil

Remember Past Lives Incense
1 part sandalwood
½ part cinnamon
½ part myrrh resin
Few drops of myrrh oil
Few drops of cinnamon oil
Few drops of cucumber oil

Spirit Presence

These next three incenses are good when you wish to invite positive energies to be present during magical rituals.

Spirit Incense 1
1 part sandalwood
1 part lavender

Burn on your altar or in your sacred space.

Spirit Incense 2
2 parts sandalwood
1 part willow bark

This incense is a good one to use (particularly outdoors) when performing rituals during the waxing Moon.

Open Eyes To Spirit World
1 part gum mastic
1 part amaranth
1 part yarrow

Visions
The next five incenses can all be used as part of rituals where you wish to make a connection with other realms.

Psychic Vision Incense
3 parts frankincense resin
1 part bay
½ part damiana

Second Sight Incense
1 part parsley
½ part hemp seeds
½ part frankincense resin

Sight Incense
2 parts gum mastic
2 parts juniper
1 part sandalwood
1 part cinnamon
1 part calamus
Few drops of patchouli oil
Few drops of ambergris oil

Vision Incense
3 parts cinquefoil
3 Parts chicory root
1 part clove

Celestial Influences

This section is probably for those of you who have chosen to travel a little further on your voyage of discovery. The incenses again are used to make a link or to enhance a specific purpose. It will depend on your own personal belief whether, for instance, you wish to use a specific incense to link with planetary energy or to use a specific incense at the times of the various Sabbats and Moon phases.

Accepted use has meant that certain woods and herbs are associated with days of the week, seasons of the year and lunar cycles. What follows is an easy-to-consult listing to enable you to get the best out of your rituals. There is nothing to stop you from mixing and matching as you so wish. You may find certain aromas more pleasurable than others, but do remember that the purpose of incense in spell-working is to affect change in your circumstances rather than simply to have something that smells nice.

Days of the Week

The incenses and oils below may be used alone or combined for your daily rituals for maximum effect. They have been recommended according to the planetary ruler of the days of the week.

Day of the Week	Planetary Influence	Aroma
Monday	Moon	Jasmine, lemon, sandalwood, Stephanotis
Tuesday	Mars	Basil, coriander, ginger, nasturtium
Wednesday	Mercury	Benzoin, clary sage, eucalyptus, lavender
Thursday	Jupiter	Clove, lemon balm, melissa, oakmoss, star anise
Friday	Venus	Cardamon, palma rosa, rose, yarrow
Saturday	Saturn	Cypress, mimosa, myrrh, patchouli
Sunday	Sun	Cedar, frankincense, neroli, rosemary

The Seasons

The following fragrances, either as plants or – where appropriate – essential oils, can be used to welcome each new season as it arrives and honour it in your personal rituals.

Spring: All sweet scents, particularly daffodil, jasmine and rose.
Summer: All spicy scents, particularly carnation, clove and ginger.
Autumn: All earthly scents, particularly oak moss, patchouli and vetiver.
Winter: All resinous and woody scents, particularly frankincense, pine and rosemary.

The following seven incenses are suitable for the various seasons and can be used either to honour the turning of the year or the ideas inherent in seasonal worship.

Spring Incense
¼ part primrose
1 part cherry

1 part rose
½ part sandalwood
Few drops of lilac oil

Few drops of rose oil
Few drops of strawberry oil

Summer Incense 1
1½ parts lavender
1 part St John's Wort
½ part mistletoe

Summer Incense 2
1 part cedar
½ part juniper
1 part sandalwood

Autumn Incense
¼ part oak
½ part pine
¼ part frankincense resin
¼ cinnamon
¼ part cloves
½ part rosemary
¼ part sage
½ part pomegranate

Winter Incense
1¼ parts lavender
½ part cloves
½ part cinnamon
¼ part benzoin resin
¼ part patchouli
¼ part mistletoe
¼ part orris root
Few drops of bergamot oil

Winter Incense 2
½ part mistletoe
¼ part holly
½ part bay
½ part oak
1 part pine
½ part cedar
Few drops of pine oil
Few drops of cedar oil

The Lunar Cycle
Incense and perfumes can be utilized during the phases of the Moon to put you in touch with lunar energy.

Sandalwood is particularly appropriate for the first quarter when the Moon's waxing enhances spirituality.
Jasmine has the full-blown energies of the Full Moon.
Lemon, which is more ethereal, is symbolic of the lessening of the Moon's influence as it wanes in the last quarter.
Camphor signifies the similarly cold New Moon.

The Elements
Traditional witchcraft dictates that you honour the four 'directions' and their appropriate Elements. Incense can also help you in this purpose, permitting you to acknowledge these aspects of spell-making.

The following four incenses are suitable for honouring the four directions or cardinal points before moving onto the ritual proper. You can then use any of the other incenses given earlier in this section, as required, for their appropriate purpose.

Air Incense
2 parts benzoin resin
1 part gum mastic
½ part lavender
¼ part wormwood
1 pinch mistletoe

Earth Incense
1 part pine
1 part thyme
Few drops patchouli oil

Fire Incense
2 parts frankincense resin
1 part dragon's blood resin
1 part red sandalwood
1 pinch saffron

Water Incense
2 parts benzoin resin
1 part myrrh resin
1 part sandalwood
Few drops of lotus oil

Planetary
These incenses can be used when you wish to call particularly on the power of the planets in your rituals. Incenses suitable for use with Neptune, Uranus and Pluto are not included, as here you might like to use your own intuition.

Sun Incense 1
3 parts frankincense resin
2 parts myrrh resin
1 part wood aloe
½ part Balm of Gilead
½ part bay
½ part carnation
Few drops of ambergris oil
Few drops of musk oil
Few drops of olive oil

Burn this incense to draw on the influences of the Sun and for spells involving promotions, friendships, healing, energy and magical power.

Sun Incense 2
3 parts frankincense resin
2 parts sandalwood
1 part bay
1 pinch saffron
Few drops of orange oil

Sun Incense 3
3 parts frankincense resin
2 parts galangal root
2 parts bay
¼ part mistletoe
Few drops of red wine
Few drops of honey

Egyptian Solar Incense
3 parts frankincense resin

1 part clove
½ part red sandalwood
½ part sandalwood
¼ part orange flowers
3 pinches of orris root

Moon Incense 1

2 parts juniper
1 part calamus
½ part orris root
¼ part camphor
Few drops of lotus oil

Moon Incense 2

4 parts sandalwood
2 parts wood aloe
1 part eucalyptus
1 part crushed cucumber seeds
1 part mugwort
½ part ranuculus blossoms
1 part selenetrope (you can
   substitute gardenia or jasmine
   if you cannot find selenetrope
   easily)
Few drops of ambergris oil

Moon Incense 3

2 parts juniper berries
1 part orris root
1 part calamus
Few drops of spirits of camphor
   or camphor
tincture or ¼ part genuine
   camphor
Few drops of lotus bouquet oil

Moon Incense 4

2 parts myrrh resin
2 parts gardenia petals
1 part rose petals

1 part lemon peel
½ part camphor
Few drops of jasmine oil

Moonfire Incense 5

1 part rose
1 part orris root
1 part bay
1 part juniper
1 part dragon's blood powder or
   resin
½ part potassium nitrate
   (saltpetre)

Burn this incense when you wish
to call on the power of the Moon
while performing divination and
love rituals. The potassium nitrate
(saltpetre) is included to make the
incense sparkle and glow. Do not
add too much though, and add it
gradually, or it will explode.

Earth Incense

2 parts pine
1 part patchouli
1 part cypress
1 pinch salt

Mercury Incense 1

2 parts benzoin resin
1 part mace
½ part marjoram
Few drops of lavender oil

Burn this incense to invoke
Mercury's powers and qualities
when performing rituals for such
things as intelligence, travel and
divination.

Mercury Incense 2
2 parts sandalwood
1 part mace
1 part marjoram
1 part mint or a few drops of
mint oil

Venus Incense 1
2 parts sandalwood
1 part benzoin resin
1 part rose petals
Few drops of rose oil
Few drops of patchouli oil

Venus Incense 2
3 parts wood aloe
1 part red rose petals
Few drops of olive oil
Few drops of musk oil
Few drops of ambergris oil

You may find it easier to mix the oils together first. Burn this for help from Venus in spells for love, healing and rituals involving women and beauty.

Mars Incense 1
2 parts galangal root
1 part coriander
1 part cloves
½ part basil
Pinch of black pepper

Mars Incense 2
2 parts dragon's blood powder or
    resin
1 part cardamom
1 part clove
1 part Grains of Paradise

This is a good incense to use if you need the assertive qualities of Mars.

Mars Incense 3
4 parts benzoin resin
1 part pine needles or resin
Scant pinch of black pepper

Burn this incense to utilize the powers and attributes of Mars or during spells involving lust, competition of any sort and anything to do with the masculine.

Jupiter Incense
1 part clove
1 part nutmeg
1 part cinnamon
½ part Balm of Gilead
½ part lemon peel

Remember that Jupiter is the planet and god of expansion, so you need to be very specific in your intent when calling upon Jupiter.

Saturn Incense 1
2 parts sandalwood resin
2 parts myrrh resin
1 part Dittany of Crete
Few drops of cypress oil
Few drops of patchouli oil

This is the recommended Saturn incense formula. Remember that Saturn does put blocks in the way, but then also encourages from behind.

Saturn Incense 2
2 parts cypress
1 part myrrh resin

1 part dittany
Few drops of patchouli oil

Ceremonial and Consecrational
Here we have put together some of the older types of incense. Some are suitable for consecrating your altar, your tools, your circle and other artefacts, while others will help strengthen the magic in the ritual itself.

Altar Incense
1 part frankincense resin
½ part myrrh resin
¼ part cinnamon

Consecration Incense
1 part mace
½ part frankincense resin
1 part benzoin resin
1 part gum arabic

This incense can be used for consecrating your sacred space as well as any tools you may need.

Ceremonial Magic Incense
1 part frankincense resin
½ part gum mastic
¼ part sandalwood

Ritual Magic Incense
2 parts frankincense resin
1 part wood aloe
Few drops of musk oil
Few drops of ambergris oil

Circle Incense
2 parts frankincense resin
1 part myrrh resin
1 part benzoin resin
½ part sandalwood

¼ part cinnamon
½ part rose
½ part bay
¼ part vervain
¼ part rosemary

Sacred Space Incense
½ part bay
½ part camphor
½ part lavender
½ part broom
½ part linden
½ part ground ivy

Crystal Purification Incense
2 parts frankincense resin
2 parts copal resin
1 part sandalwood
1 part rosemary

This incense is used when consecrating your crystals so that they work magically for you. It 'wipes' all other vibration and aligns the crystal with your purpose.

Offertory Incense
2 parts frankincense resin
1 part myrrh resin
1 part cinnamon

½ part rose petals
½ part vervain

Burn this incense while honouring the goddesses and gods and also as an offering during rituals.

Talisman and Amulet Consecration Incense
2 parts frankincense resin
1 part cypress
1 part tobacco
½ part ash

Talisman Consecration
2 parts frankincense resin
1 part cypress
1 part ash leaves
1 part tobacco
1 pinch valerian
1 pinch alum
1 pinch of asafoetida powder

Temple Incense
3 parts frankincense resin
2 parts myrrh resin
Few drops of lavender oil
Few drops of sandalwood oil

Burn this incense in your sacred space or grove. You can also use this as a general magical incense or to consecrate your shrine.

Universal Incense
3 parts frankincense resin
2 parts benzoin resin
1 part myrrh resin
1 part sandalwood
1 part rosemary

Burn this incense for all positive magical purposes. If used for negative magical goals, it will cancel out the spell or ritual.

The use of incense becomes such a part of everyday life that you will often find yourself feeling quite bereft when you are not within your own personally enhanced environment. The section that follows on oils will give you an idea of oils that you can carry with you on your travels to enhance your environment wherever you are.

OILS

At various points in the book, you will read of the many oils that can be utilized as adjuncts to the various types of magic. They are an easy way of using plants in magical workings, particularly when space is at a premium.

Below are some oils that should be part of every magical practitioner's way of working. For your reference their Latin names are also given. All of them are simple to acquire and even though the initial expense may seem to be prohibitive, if they are stored according to directions, they will last for some time.

Cinnamon *(Cinnamomum zeylanicum)*, with its warm vibration, brings into our hearts love from higher realms, if only we allow it. The warm glow of cinnamon exudes right through space and time, transforming sadness into happiness. Cinnamon was used in China in 2700BC, and was known to the Egyptians by 1500BC.

Clary sage *(Salvia sclarea)* has benefits for both the physical and mental aspects of mankind, teaching us to be content with what we have. It brings prosperity of the spirit, and the realization that most problems arise in our imagination. This herb lifts the spirit and links with eternal wisdom.

Frankincense *(Boswellia carterii)* holds some of the wisdom of the universe, both spiritual and meditative. Able to cleanse the most negative of influences, it operates as a spiritual prop in a wide range of circumstances. It works far beyond the auric field, affecting the very subtle realms of energy and adapting the spiritual state. Frankincense is sometimes called olibanum.

Geranium *(Pelargonium graveolens)* resonates with Mother Earth and all that is feminine. It typifies the archetypal energy of Goddess culture. Its energy is transformational and as such it must always be used with respect. It comforts, opens our hearts and heals pain.

Jasmine *(Jasminum officinale)* provides us with our personal sanctuary and allows us access to a greater understanding of the spirit. It is said that jasmine brings the angelic kingdom within our reach, thus allowing us to be the best we can. It gives understanding and acceptance of the true meaning of spirituality.

Lavender *(Lavendula angustifolia)* is caring and nurturing. By allowing the heavenly energies close to the physical, it brings about healing and thus signifies the protective love of Mother Earth. Gentle and relaxing, it changes the perception to enable one to make progress. Lavender will not allow negative emotion to remain present within the aura for long.

Myrrh *(Commiphora myrrha)* signifies the pathway of the soul, allowing us to let go when the time is right. Wounds of body, mind and spirit are healed by myrrh and it brings realization that we no longer need to carry our burdens, releasing them from deep within. When combined with other oils, it enhances – and is enhanced by – them.

Neroli *(Citrus aurantium)* is one of the most precious essential oils, its vibration being one of the highest. It is pure spirit and is loving and peaceful. It brings self-recognition and respite because it allows development of a new perspective, allowing us to cast off the bonds of old ways of relating and to develop unconditional love. In magical working it allows one to be a pure channel.

Nutmeg *(Myristica fragrans)* helps us to reconnect with the higher realms of spirit and to experience again a sense of spiritual wonderment. When the spirit is affected by disappointment, spiritual pain and displacement, nutmeg works to bring hopes, dreams and prayers back into focus. At one time, nutmeg was given to people who were thought to be possessed by spirits.

Rose absolute *(Rosa damascene)* In India the 'Great Mother' was known as the 'Holy Rose' and this personification reveals just how profound the effects of this perfume are when used magically. Said to be the perfume of the guardians or messengers who guide us in times of need, it is a soul fragrance which allows us to access the divine mysteries. It is associated with the true needs of the human heart.

Rosemary *(Rosmarinus officinalis)* reminds us of our purpose and of our own spiritual journey. It opens the human spirit to understanding and wisdom, and encourages confidence and clarity of purpose. It cleanses the aura and enables us to assist others in their search for spirituality.

Sandalwood *(Santalum album)* acts as a bridge between heaven and earth and allows us to make contact with divine beings. It enables us to be calm enough to hear the music of the spheres and beings us into balance with the cosmos. It clarifies our strength of conviction.

Ylang ylang *(Cananga odorata)* gives a new appreciation of the sensual side of our being. It balances the spirit so that we can be open to pleasures of the physical realm while still appreciating spiritual passions. It brings a sense of completion to the tasks that belong to the physical realm. Used magically, it achieves a balanced manifestation.

Ritual Bathing

One way in which essential oils can be used is in preparation for ritual and spell-making. Magical practitioners know that ritual bathing is an intrinsic part of any working and that they should come to their work as pure and unsullied as possible. Purification baths are not about personal cleanliness, but are part of acknowledging that the power and energy will flow more freely through a cleansed 'vessel'. There is a method for a ritual bath here, as well as a way of preparing bath salts.

Essential oils have within them all four of the Elements, a fact that many people like to acknowledge. They are products of the Earth, having been distilled they flow (Water), they will burn (Fire) and they release perfume (Air). When the water and salt – which also has a cleansing effect – of a ritual bath are combined, we have a perfect vehicle for cleansing our subtle energies.

Below are some oils for you to use in your ritual bath. Different blends have different effects, depending on the individual, so experiment until you find the one that suits you best. Make sure whichever oils you choose are well blended and use in the quantities indicated.

Ritual Bath Oils
Neroli 3 drops
Orange 1 drop
Petitgrain 2 drops
Myrtle 3 drops
Clary sage 1 drop
Lemon 1 drop
Rosemary 2 drops
Eucalyptus 1 drop
Lavender 3 drops

Chamomile 3 drops
Mandarin 3 drops
Frankincense 4 drops
Lemon 2 drops
Rose 3 drops
Neroli 3 drops

Essential oil blends

Essential oils can be used in spells to generate a higher vibration. The following blends can be used for anointing candles and for blessing objects as well as for personal use. Ideally, when you combine oils, they should be well shaken together and left for at least an hour so that the synergy begins to work. Synergy takes place when the subtle vibrations of the oils blend to create a further vibration, therefore enhancing their energy.

If you are intending on using essential oils as massage oils, remember to use a carrier oil such as almond or grapeseed. Neat essential oils should, as a rule, never be used directly on the skin or ingested.

Romance Magnet Oil
2 drops ylang ylang oil
2 drops sandalwood oil
2 drops clary sage oil

To attract love, rub romance magnet oil onto a pink candle and then burn it for three hours a day, every day, until the person makes an advance. The candle should be snuffed rather than blown out.

Lover's Oil
5 drops rosewood oil
5 drops rosemary oil
3 drops tangerine oil
3 drops lemon oil

Lover's oil may be used to enhance a relationship in all sorts of ways. Consecrate a candle with lover's oil and light it half an hour before your date arrives.

Marriage Oil
2 drops frankincense oil
3 drops cypress oil
2 drops sandalwood oil

This combination of oils is used to reinforce a marriage relationship, whether the union is good or not. It may also be used to help steer a relationship towards marriage or further commitment. Simply burn a pink or lilac-coloured candle anointed with marriage oil when you and your partner are together.

Desire Oil
3 drops lavender oil
3 drops orange oil
1 drop lemon oil

Desire oil is meant to entice another person to want you. If someone already does, but needs a little pushing, a red, orange, pink, blue, or white candle should be anointed and lit when the two of you are together. If you love someone and they are showing no response, speak their name as you light a candle blessed with desire oil.

Allow the candles to burn for two hours before you snuff them out.

Repeat, until the person reacts.

Dream Potion
10 drops jasmine oil
10 drops nutmeg oil
3 drops clary sage

This oil can be used to enhance the atmosphere of the bedroom before sleep. It is best burnt in an aromatherapy lamp rather than being used as a body oil.

To Strengthen an Existing Relationship
10 drops rose oil
10 drops sandalwood oil
5 drops lavender oil

This oil can be used as a perfume or to scent the atmosphere.

Aphrodisiac Oil
Use the following potent mixture as a perfume or added to 50 ml (2 fl oz) of unscented massage oil (such as grapeseed or almond oil, which make a good base) and have fun!

10 drops ylang ylang
2 drops cinnamon
5 drops sweet orange
3 drops jasmine oil
10 drops patchouli
10 drops sandalwood
10 drops ylang ylang

Oils for Ritual Work
The following oil blends can all be used in ritual work.

Sacred Space Blend
20 drops juniper berry oil
10 drops frankincense oil
10 drops sandalwood oil
5 drops rosemary oil
2 drops nutmeg oil

This is a good blend to use when you need to create a sacred space or magical circle. Burnt in an aromatherapy lamp it clears and enhances the atmosphere.

Prosperity Blend
Equal parts of patchouli and basil oil

This combination creates the right vibration for prosperity of all sorts (not necessarily financial).

Altar Oil Blend
4 parts frankincense
3 parts myrrh
1 part galangal
1 part vervain
1 part lavender

This blend is one that can be used to anoint your altar, if you use one, or to diffuse around your sacred space at regular intervals, before you undertake any ritual, to purify and empower the space.

Goddess Oil Blend
10 drops neroli oil

5 drops nutmeg oil
10 drops sandalwood oil
10 drops jasmine oil

When you invoke the Goddess, this oil is wonderful for allowing your vibration to meet with hers at any time of the year.

Protection Blend
10 drops juniper oil
5 drops vetiver oil
5 drops basil oil
2 drops clove oil

Should you feel that you are in need of protection, this oil can be burnt in an aromatherapy burner or sprinkled on a tissue and placed on a warm radiator.

Using Essential Oils in the Auric Field

As they begin working magically, almost all practitioners will find that they become more sensitive to the vibrations of the ordinary, everyday world. A crowded train, for instance, when you are bombarded by the various vibrations of your fellow travellers, can be very difficult to handle. This difficulty arises because your own particular 'force field', called the aura – which you carry with you always – begins to vibrate at a different level than the one to which you are accustomed and do not notice on an everyday level.

If you begin to do a great deal of magical work, you must learn to protect yourself, perhaps from onslaughts of negativity or subtle vibrations over which others have no control. Always remember that you have at your disposal the means for control and it should become a regular part of your routine to enhance your own aura and to protect that of others. Essential oils can help you to do this.

Methods of Using Oils for Protective Purposes

Method 1 Put just one drop of your chosen pure essential oil in the centre of your palm and rub your hands together. In this instance the oil is used neat. Holding your hands about 10 cm (4 in) away from your body, smooth around the outside of this space, starting from the top of your head down to your feet and then back up again. Make sure you have covered every part that you can reach of this very subtle body. This is also known as protecting your aura.

Method 2 Use your chosen oils in a spray or diffuser, spraying around your body and over the top of your head again, ensuring that you cover the whole area. Prepare your oils in advance, combining them as necessary. Leave them for a week in a quiet, dark place away from electrical equipment. On the eighth day use a new fragrance sprayer, preferably a glass bottle, add about 25 ml (1 fl oz) of the purest water available and the essential oils and shake the sprayer vigorously. This can also be used to protect your sacred space or immediate environment.

Energizing Oils
The following are energizing oils and will give a real lift to your power (the proportions used can be to your own personal preference):

Basil, Coriander, Eucalyptus, Fir, Lemon, Peppermint, Spruce

Harmonizing Oils
The oils in this next group are used for establishing harmony, both in person who uses them and in the atmosphere:

Clary sage, Fennel, Geranium, Ginger, Juniper, Lavender, Mandarin, Orange, Petitgrain

Following is a selection of recipes based on all these oils:

Cleansing blend
Pine 4 drops
Lemon 3 drops
Basil 3 drops
Fir needle 5 drops
Spruce 5 drops

This blend cleanses the aura, as suggested above, and gives an idea of the correct proportions to use.

Aura harmonization
Geranium 4 drops
Juniper 2 drops
Orange 6 drops
Fennel 1 drop
Petitgrain 6 drops

This blend is particularly useful when you wish to cleanse and harmonize your aura.

Connecting with the Essential
The oils below help you to make a connection with your spiritual self, the essential you:

Frankincense, Rose, Neroli, Linden blossom, Jasmine

Linking blend
Galbanum 1 drop
Frankincense 4 drops
Jasmine 2 drops
Neroli 7 drops
Rose 7 drops

Sacred Space

If you are going to be carrying out a fair number of rituals or spells, you will really need a sacred space or altar along with various other altar furnishings. Whether your altar is inside or outside does not matter. To set it up indoors, your altar and/or sacred space should preferably be in a quiet place in the home, where it will not be disturbed and where candles can be burned safely.

The space first needs to be dedicated to the purpose of magical working. You can do this by first brushing the area clean with an ordinary brush, concentrating your thoughts on cleansing the space as you work physically to bring this about. Mentally cleanse the space three times, imagining doing it once for the physical world, once for the emotional space and once spiritually.

If you wish, you may sprinkle the whole area with water and with salt (which represents the earth). You might perhaps also burn incense such as benzoin, jasmine or frankincense to clear the atmosphere. Think of the space as somewhere you would entertain an honoured guest in your home – you would wish the room you use to be as welcoming as possible. You will later use your besom to keep the sacred space clear.

If you travel a lot or are pushed for space, you might dedicate a tray or special piece of wood or china for ceremonial working. This, along with your candles and incense, can then be kept together in a small box or suitcase. Otherwise, you could dedicate a table especially for the purpose. Ideally, you should not need to pack up each time.

You will also need a 'fine cloth' – the best you can afford – to cover the surface. Place your cloth on your chosen surface and spend some quiet time just thinking about its purpose. You may, if you wish, have different cloths for different purposes or perhaps have one basic cloth, which is then 'dressed' with the appropriate colour for each ritual.

Setting up your altar

To turn your dressed table into a proper altar, you will need as basics the following objects:

1. Two candles with candle holders – you might like to think of one representing the female principle and one the male. In addition, you may also choose candles of a colour suitable for the ritual or spell you are working.

2. An incense holder, and incense suitable for the particular working.
3. A representation of the deity or deities you prefer to work with. An image of the Goddess, for instance, could be anything from a statue of the Chinese Goddess of Compassion, Kuan Yin, to seashells, chalices, bowls, or certain stones that symbolize the womb or motherhood.
4. A small vase for flowers or fresh herbs.

As already mentioned in the Principles and Components section, there are other objects that you are likely to need for your ceremonial working. Briefly, these are:

1. An athame, which is a sacred knife for ceremonial use; it should never be used for anything else.
2. A white-handled knife (called a boline) for cutting branches, herbs, and so on.
3. A burin, which is a sharp-pointed instrument for inscribing magical objects such as candles.
4. A small earthenware or ceramic bowl, or a small cauldron, for mixing ingredients.
5. A bowl of water.
6. A bowl of salt or sand, representing Earth.
7. A consecrated cloth, or a pentacle, on which to place dedicated objects.

Some people additionally use bells to summon the powers of the Elements, while others have additional candles with the colours representing both themselves and the work they wish to do. You can also have other items on your altar, such as crystals, amulets and talismans.

You can do what you wish with your own altar. You should have thought through very carefully the logical or emotional reasons for including whatever you have there. You might, for instance, choose to have differing representations of the Earth Mother from diverse religions, or include a pretty gift to establish a psychic link with the person who gave it to you.

Dedicating your altar

Now you have turned your space into an altar, dedicate it in such a way that it will support any workings you may choose to do. One good way is to dedicate it to the principle of the Greater Good – that none may be harmed by anything that you may do. (Remember that traditionally any harm you instigate deliberately will return to you threefold, particularly when it comes from such a sacred space.) It will depend on your basic belief just how you choose to dedicate the altar further, perhaps to the Moon deity and all her manifestations, perhaps to the gods of power.

Try to put as much passion and energy into the dedication as you can, and remember to include a prayer for protection of your sacred space. Some people will need to cast a circle each time they do a working, while others will feel that just by setting the altar up in the way suggested, the space is consecrated henceforth. If you wish to follow the principles of feng shui rather than Wicca within your work, your placings will be slightly different, as they will also be if you choose to follow the tenets of other religions.

However, whatever you do, you should take care to dedicate all of your tools and altar furnishings to the purpose in hand. You are empowering them and making them usable only in ritual and magical work. If you try to use them for any other purpose, you will negate that magical power.

Consecrating altar objects

If you are not using completely new objects as the basic furnishings (such as candle holders) on your altar, you should cleanse them before you dedicate them to your purpose. Treat them in the same way as you would any crystals you use, by soaking them overnight in salt water to remove anyone else's vibrations and then standing them in sunshine (or moonshine) for at least twelve hours, to charge them with the appropriate energy.

When you are ready, hold each object and allow your own energy to flow into it, followed by the energy of your idea of Ultimate Power. (That way you make a very powerful link between yourself, the object and the Ultimate.) Ask this Power to bless the object and any working you may do with it, and perceive yourself as truly a medium or channel for the energy.

Hopefully, each time you use any of the objects, you will immediately be able to reinforce that link rather than having to reestablish it. It is like a refrain continually running in the background. Now place the objects on your altar in whatever way feels right for you.

Finally, if you wish, create and cast your circle (see below) so that it includes yourself and your altar. The magic circle defines the ritual area, holds in personal power and shuts out all distractions and negative energies. You now have a sacred space set up, which is your link to the powers that be. Again it is a matter of personal choice as to whether you choose to rededicate your altar and what it contains on a regular basis. Use your intuition to decide if the link requires renewal.

Casting a circle

Purify yourself first. You can do this by meditating, or taking a ritual bath. One way is to try to keep the water flowing, possibly by leaving the bath plug half in, or by having a shower. This reinforces the idea of washing away any impurities so you are not sitting in your own psychic rubbish. Ideally, your towel – if you choose to use one – should be clean and used only for the purpose of your ritual bath.

Wear something special if you can, something that you only wear during a ritual or working – perhaps your robes. You can always add a pretty scarf or a throw in the correct colour for your working. This sets apart spell-working from everyday bathing and dressing.

Decide on the extent of your circle, which should be formed in front of your altar. Purify this space by sprinkling the area with water followed by salt – both of these should have been blessed or consecrated with simple words.

Sit quietly for as long as you can inside the area that will become your circle. Imagine a circle of light surrounding you. This light could be white, blue or purple. If you are in a hurry and cannot purify and cleanse fully, reinforce the circle of light by visualizing it suffused with the appropriate colour for your working.

Circle the light around, above and below you in a clockwise direction, like the representation of an atom. Feel it as a sphere or as a cone of power. Sense the power. Remember that you can create a 'doorway' through which your magical energy may exit. You should always feel warm and peaceful within your circle. As time goes on, you will be able to differentiate between the various energies.

Use your own personal chant or form of words, according to your own belief system, to consecrate your circle and banish all evil and negative energy, forbidding anything harmful to enter your space. Remember, you are always safe within your circle if you command it to be so.

If you wish, invite the gods and goddesses to attend your circle and magical working. Relax and be happy.

You can use objects on the ground to show the boundaries of the circle, such as candles, crystals, cord, stones, flowers or incense. The circle is formed from personal power. This may be felt and visualized as streaming from the body to form a bubble made of mist, or a circle of light. You can use the athame or your hands to direct this power.

The cardinal points of the compass may be denoted with lit candles, often white or purple. Alternatively, place a green candle at the north point of the circle, yellow candle at the east, red candle at the south and blue candle at the west. The altar stands in the centre of the circle, facing north in the direction of power.

An Alternative Method of Circle Casting
This method probably owes more to the practices of Wicca than any other way, though you do not have to be Wiccan to use it.

YOU WILL NEED
Besom
Ritual tools (see pages 16-19)
Candle to represent your working
Altar candles to represent the Goddess and God
Any of the ceremonial or consecrational incenses here
Heatproof dish for the incense
Compass (to work out directions)
Candle snuffer

METHOD
Cleanse the sacred space symbolically with the besom.

Place the altar in the centre of the circle facing north.

Set up the altar as described above.

Light the candles on the altar.

Start with the candle representing the Goddess on
the left, then the God on the right. In the middle,
follow with the candle which represents your magical
working. Light the incense.

Move towards the northern edge of the area
you are enclosing.

Hold your left hand out, palm down, at waist level.
Point your fingers toward the edge of the circle you are
creating. (You can, of course, use your athame if you
have consecrated it.)

See and feel the energy flowing out from your fingertips
(or the athame), and slowly walk the circle, clockwise.
Think of the energy that your body is generating.

Continue to move clockwise, gradually increasing
your pace as you do so.

Move faster until you feel the energy flowing within you.

The energy will move with you as you release it.

Sense your personal power creating a sphere of energy
around the altar. When this is firmly established, call on
the Elements which rule the four directions.

*Your circle is now consecrated and ready for you to use for whatever
magical purpose you need. You will require the candle snuffer when
you close your circle after your magical working.*

Ending your magical working

As well as all the preparations necessary for successful magical working,
it is equally important to finish off correctly. When you have finished
your ritual or working, remind yourself that you are as pure a channel for
the energies that you have called upon as possible. These energies *must*
be returned whence they came, so visualize them passing through you
and being returned to where they belong. At the same time, remember
that you are blessed by these energies and by the fact that you have used
them with good intent.

Closing a Circle

Thank the Elements' rulers, if you have called upon them, for attending
the ritual.

If you used ritual tools, holding your athame, stand at the north.
Pierce the circle's wall with the blade at waist level. If you wish, simply
use your index finger to achieve the same end.

Move clockwise around the circle. Visualize its power being
sucked back into the knife or your finger. Sense the sphere of energy
withdrawing and dissipating.

Let the outside world slowly make itself felt in your consciousness.
As you come back to the north again, the energy of the circle should
have disappeared. If it has not, simply repeat the actions.

If you have laid items to mark out the circle, remove them. If you have used salt and water, you may save the excess salt for future uses, but pour the water onto the bare earth. Bury any incense ashes.

Put out the candles. Start with those that have marked the cardinal compass points, followed by any others used.

Next put out the one representing the God energy and finally the Goddess candle. Never blow them out (some say this dissipates the energy). Either snuff or pinch them out.

You may leave the candles to burn out on their own if you wish.

Put away your tools if you are not able to leave your altar in place.

The significance of Colour

Colour is something that, over time, you will use as a natural adjunct in your magical workings. It can be used in your robes, to dress your altar, or in your candles as representative of the vibration you wish to introduce. By and large, the colours you choose for your workings will be those appropriate for your intention (the purpose of your spell).

There are other uses of colour in magic as well. Some simple colour symbolism is listed below.

Silver is almost always associated with the lunar goddesses and workings with the Moon, whereas **white** symbolizes purity, chastity, spirituality, transformation and transmutation. It is said to contain within it all the other colours, so always use white if you have nothing else available. Use it also when you want focus and a protective influence.

Purple, indigo and **violet** are the royal colours and are therefore associated with wisdom and vision, dignity and fame. They are often used when honouring the Goddess in her aspect of Crone and the God as King, according to some traditions of magic. These colours command respect and promote psychic and mental healing. Purple connects with true creativity, with the mystic and with spirituality and is also to do with one's proper place within the overall scheme of things.

Sky blue signifies communication, not just between people, but also between the realms so is good for meditative practices and also for help with study and learning. It is also used to symbolize Water. Other shades of blue signify peace; strength; calm; recognition of the real self and the ability to express wisdom.

Green, which belongs to Venus, promotes love, fertility, beauty, wealth, prosperity and harmony – symbolizing balance and self-knowledge, that is, knowing our capabilities. Associated with the Earth in its guise of the Green Man and with the Great Mother in her nurturing form, it suggests emotional healing and growth.

Gold and **yellow** represent vitality, strength and rejuvenation. They are used to promote physical healing, hope and happiness. Yellow inspires rational thought and strong will. It is also an emotional colour in the sense that it represents your relationship with the outer self and the world in which you live. Related to the Sun gods and the Element of Air, both gold and yellow may also be used for protection.

Orange has a healing vibration, particularly of relationships. It is also associated with material success and legal matters. A highly creative vibration, it often relates to childhood and emotional stability as well as imagination.

Red is recognized as being symbolic of passion and sexual potency and intensity. It is usually associated with Fire, with the quality of courage and with healing of the blood and heart.

Pink signifies friendship, love, fidelity and the healing of emotions. It also symbolizes creativity and innocence and is associated with the Goddess in her aspect of Maiden.

Brown promotes the healing of the Earth, symbolizes the hearth and home, and is also connected with the animal kingdom. It can also be used for the blending of several intentions.

Black is not a colour but is the absence of both light and colour. It can therefore be used to banish negativity. It is often seen as the colour of the Goddess in her Wise Woman form.

Constructing spells

Traditionally, spells, formulas and rituals were recorded in the Grimoire which, of late, has become known as the Book of Shadows. There is often controversy over whether one's magical book should be called a Grimoire or a Book of Shadows. Really it depends on which tradition of magic you have been taught.

The word Grimoire simply means 'a book of learning'. It came to mean the records kept by true practitioners of magic, as they wrote down the secret keys they discovered as they progressed along the path of initiation. The best-known Grimoire was the translation of one made widely available at the beginning of the 20th century – that of King Solomon. This book was of great antiquity and traditionally is seen as the magical key to the Kabbalah. In truth, it was the key to the mysteries and has since formed the basis of other magical systems.

The first Book of Shadows is said to have been written by Gerald Gardner as he developed modern Wicca in the 1940s. The Book of Shadows does not serve as a diary, but reflects religious rituals, their modifications and any other workings that need to be recorded.

Both books were traditionally secret writings, often written in coded language. The Book of Shadows follows the same principle, although obviously with modern communication, much of what used to be hidden is more readily available.

Most solitary practitioners will treasure the records of their workings, whether they choose to call it a Book of Shadows or a Grimoire. Either book becomes part of a rich tradition. Any self-respecting practitioner will both want and need to keep a record of all of these aspects of magic for future reference. You will need to find an easy way of remembering what you have done. Utilizing the worksheets and the respective headings below will help you to do this.

These can also be used, should you wish, with modern technology. Computer documents can be tremendously helpful in keeping records in a fashion that is suitable for passing on to other people.

Spells and Formulas Record Sheet

Type of Spell or Formula: This should state very clearly what the type of spell is, for example blessing, binding, and so on. When developing formulas, you need to be clear as to the exact purpose.

Date and Time Made: This gives a cross reference should you wish to use the correct planetary hours or magical days.

Reference: You should develop your own system of reference; this might be, for instance, according to the time of year or alphabetically. Do also remember to keep safely somewhere a record of how you have developed your reference system, so that others may benefit from your experience.

Astrological Phase: If you have an interest in astrology you will probably want to record where the planets are when you prepare the spell or formula. A decent ephemeris (list of planetary positions) can be of great help here, though there are also many sources of information on the internet.

Specific Purpose: You should always state the specific purpose of the spell or formula very clearly. This is partly because it helps to focus your own mind, but also because it leaves no one in any doubt as to your intentions. Should you have more than one main purpose, you should also record these.

List of Ingredients and/or Supplies Needed: Having all your ingredients to hand ensures that you are working with maximum efficiency and are not misusing or needing to adjust the energy by leaving the sacred space. Also, when you repeat a working you will need to replicate what you did the first time; even one small change in ingredients can make a tremendous difference to the outcome.

Specific Location Required: You may well need to perform some spells within a certain area or setting. Also you may discover that your own energy responds to some locations better than others.

Date, Time and Astrological Phase when Used: In all probability you will not want all your spells to take effect at the time you cast them. Let us suppose you have applied for a job and wish your spell to work at the time of interview. You would need to carefully calculate the date, time and astrological phase of the interview as well as the time you are actually casting your spell, and incorporate both into your working.

Results: Record carefully all aspects of results you feel are associated with your working. This record should include how successful you consider the spell to be and how it might be improved. There will be some unexpected results, some that appear not to give a tangible result and others which come into play some time after they were expected.

Deities Invoked during Preparation and/or Use: Often a particular god can be helpful in bringing about a needed result for a spell. You will choose the most appropriate for your purpose and can always petition a different one at another time.

Step-by-Step Instructions for Preparations and/or Use: Often, when spell-working, movements and words are intuitive and instinctive; the more you are able to remember what you did, the more likely you are to achieve similar results. Also, should you require them for someone to work on your behalf or to undertake someone else's magical training, you will have an exact record.

Additional Notes: Here you should record for each occasion anything that seems strange, bizarre or noteworthy, so that you know what to expect next time.

In each of the spells throughout this book there is a list of ingredients and special articles which may be required to achieve a result for that particular spell. Because each individual brings their own energy into the process, you may find that you intuitively want to change something, whether that is an ingredient, a container or the words used. This is absolutely fine, and means that your spell has a very personal feel to it.

Throughout the preceding sections there is information on many subjects and aspects of spell-working. You now have enough knowledge to permit you to develop your magical self. The second part of this book gives you some spells to try out that represent only a small selection of the wealth of opportunities available to you.

Part 2

THE
SPELLS

What is a Spell?

In ancient pagan communities the elders, or wise ones, had, by their very experience, an awareness of custom and a firm grasp of what had previously worked when trying to gain control over Mother Nature and other powers they did not fully understand. They had access to certain knowledge (and therefore power) that was not readily available to the ordinary individual.

The ancients recognized that words spoken in a certain way, according to custom, seemed to have more of an effect than those spoken on the spur of the moment. As a consequence, their words would have more power, yet the same words spoken by the uninitiated or those who did not understand, did not seem to have the same result.

There are three important aspects when reciting a spell. The first is that words spoken with intensity and passion do have a power all of their own. The next is that the speaker also has a power and an energy which, with practice, he or she may learn to use effectively. The third component, the forces and powers belonging to that which is 'beyond the human being' also have a tremendous power and are called upon, used or directed for a specific purpose. The use of all three of these aspects gives a very powerful spell indeed.

There are several kinds of spell, each of which requires a different kind of approach.

Love spells
Many people's first thought in this context is of love spells – ways of making another person find them sexually attractive and desirable. In theory, love spells should be unconditional and this type should be entirely unselfish and free from self-interest. However, most of the time they obviously cannot be so, unless they are performed by a third party, someone outside the longed-for relationship who is totally dispassionate about the outcome.

To try to influence someone else directly may well go against the ethics of many practitioners and magicians, though such spells do tend to be the stock-in-trade of many Eastern practitioners. Anyone who wishes to experiment with love spells needs to be aware that such spells come under the category of bidding spells and therefore must be used carefully. Love spells are often accompanied by gifts or love philtres, which are also meant to have an effect on the recipient.

Bidding spells

These are spells where the spell-maker commands a particular thing to happen, but without the co-operation of those involved. Trying to make someone do something which they do not want to do, or which goes against their natural inclination, obviously requires a great deal of power and energy and can possibly misfire, causing the originator of the spell a good deal of difficulty.

For this reason, it is wise to preface such spells with words to signify that the outcome will only be in accord with the Greater Good – that is, that in the overall scheme of things no one will be harmed in any way whatsoever. This ensures that the intent behind the spell is of the purest and that there is not any maliciousness within the practitioner. It means that an able and responsible practitioner must choose their words carefully, even when they are not casting a spell.

One type of bidding spell that is allowable is when a curse or 'hex' is being removed. A hex is a spell that ill-wishes someone and in many cases binds the recipient in some way. A curse is a spell with a much more generalized effect. To remove such a negative spell, it is usual to turn it around and send the malign energy back to the person who summoned it in the first place. You simply command the energy to return from whence it came.

Blessings

These might be counted either as prayers or spells and need a passionate concentration on bringing, for instance, peace of mind or healing to the recipient. They hold no danger for the practitioner but are sometimes more difficult to appreciate since they tend to be more general than other types of magical work. They may be thought of in terms of a positive energy from beyond the practitioner, being channelled towards a specific purpose.

Saying grace before a meal is a form of blessing preceded by an offer of praise and a prayer of thankfulness, an acknowledgement of a gift. The food is enhanced by the act and the blessing is given by drawing on the power vested in the knowledgeable expert. Thus one practitioner may call on the nature gods whereas another might call on the power of Jesus Christ.

Healing spells and charms

Within this type of spell it is wise to go beyond the presenting symptoms and to ask for healing on all levels of existence – physical, mental and spiritual – because the practitioner may not have the knowledge or correct information to enable him to diagnose a condition correctly. The natural energies and specific vibrations are enhanced by invocations, incantations and blessings wherever appropriate.

Frequently, objects such as crystals are charged with energy and power to focus healing or other energies in a quite specific way, often to remind the patient's body of its own ability to heal itself.

Invocations

These call on what is believed to be the ultimate source of power, which differs from spell to spell. Quite literally, they call up that power and ask for permission to use this influence for a stated purpose. Meddling with this power and calling up negative forces is extremely unwise and very foolish.

Spells for selfish personal power or to gain power over others will often backfire on the unwary and may cause damage to the individual who casts them. Invocations of positive forces can do no harm, except that the results can sometimes be highly disconcerting due to the sheer energy created, although the eventual outcome may be good.

Incantations

This type of spell prepares the magical worker and his helpers for further work by heightening their awareness. It does not set out to call up the powers, but appeals to gods, goddesses, powers of nature and so on for help.

Chanting, prayer and hymns are in many ways incantations, particularly when the intent is stated with some passion. An incantation is often very beautiful and rhythmic. Music has always been an efficient way of heightening awareness and altering states of consciousness.

The Elements

In most systems of magical working you will find mentioned the four (or sometimes five) Elements, often in conjunction with their directions or, as they are known in magic, quarters of the universe or cardinal points. Together and separately they are extremely powerful sources of energy and can give a tremendous boost to your spell-making.

The four Elements are energies, and manifestations of energy, that make up the entire universe. They also influence our personalities and therefore what we do. Magical working calls to each elemental kingdom and its ruler to protect each cardinal point and its properties. Each Element has an intrinsic power and is known for having certain qualities, natures, moods and magical purposes. Each also has positive and negative traits.

Earth, Air, Fire and Water are the four Elements and you may well find that you work best using one of them in particular. People drawn to candle magic, for instance, are using mainly the Element of Fire, while those who work with incense are using Air with a fair smattering of Earth in the herbs and resins.

The fifth Element is that of spirit, which is the 'binding principle' behind everything. Sometimes known as aether, it is, on the whole, intangible, yet is that which makes everything happen. You are both its representative and its channel, so in using the other Elements in magical working you have a responsibility to act wisely and well.

Earth

Traditionally the direction of this Element is north and the colour normally associated with Earth is green. It is represented on the altar usually by salt or sand. Crystals, because they are totally natural substances, can also be used.

When invoking Earth and the powers of the north, you are looking for recovery and healing and perhaps trying to find answers to questions. These powers deal with gaining knowledge, blessing, creating and shielding. When working within a magical circle, this is the first corner or quarter on which you call for protection.

The principal nature spirits of the Earth are called gnomes. They are said to live underground and guard the earth's treasures. Other groups within the earth's nature spirits ruled by the god Pan are brownies, dryads, Earth spirits, elves and satyrs.

Air

The direction of this Element is east and the colour usually associated with it is yellow. Incense is often used to represent Air, since the movement of the air can be seen in the incense smoke.

When you are looking for inspiration, need new ideas or perhaps to break free from the past or undesired situations, you would use this Element. The quality associated with it is that of thinking or the use of the intellect. When working in a magical circle, Air is the second quarter on which you call for protection.

The sylphs are the Air spirits; their Element has the most subtle energy of the four. They are said to live on the tops of mountains and are volatile and changeable. They are usually perceived with wings and look like cherubs or fairies. One of their tasks is said to be to help humans receive inspiration.

Fire

Fire is the Element of the south and is usually represented by a candle or a cauldron with a fire inside. Its colour is red and its associations are to do with power, determination and passionate energy.

You would call upon this Element for protection from evil forces, cleansing and creativity. The quality associated with Fire is 'doing' and it is a male principle. It is the third quarter or cardinal point on which you call for protection when working in a magical circle.

Without salamanders, the spirit of Fire, it is said that physical fire cannot exist. They have been seen as sparks or small balls of light, but most often they are perceived as being lizard-like in shape and about 30 cm or more in length. They are considered the strongest and most powerful of all the Elementals. As nature spirits they are greatly affected by the way that mankind thinks. Out of control, salamanders can be considered dangerous.

Water

Water is the Element of the west and is represented by a bowl of water or a goblet of wine or fruit juice. Its colour is blue and, because it represents the giving of life, it is associated with the Elements of sea, rain, snow and rivers.

When you need cleansing, revitalizing, the removal of curses or hexes or change of any sort, you will call upon Water. It is to do with emotions, right through from the most basic passions to the most elevated forms of belief. It is predominantly feminine. It is the fourth and final quarter that you invoke in any magical circle.

The undines are the Elemental beings connected with Water and are beautiful and very graceful. The nymph is frequently found in a fountain and the mythical mermaid belongs to the ocean. Some undines inhabit waterfalls, others live in rivers and lakes. Smaller undines are often seen as winged beings that people have mistakenly called fairies.

Spirit

When you feel you are sufficiently adept at using the other Elements, you may begin to use spirit – the fifth Element. This has no special space but is everywhere. It should never ever be used negatively because, particularly when you are weak and tired, it can rebound on you.

You may well find that you instinctively link strongly with the life force as spirit, in which case you are probably succeeding in bringing all the Elements together within yourself. There is no particular colour associated with spirit – perception is all-important. If you choose to represent spirit on the altar, you may do so however you wish. You are free to use your intuition and you must have a very strong awareness of your reason for choosing that particular symbol.

Different Types of Magic

Elemental

In this particular type of magic the Elements of Fire, Earth, Air and Water are given their own directional focus to create added power and give extra energy to your spells. You will no doubt find that you tend to favour one particular direction but you should be able to use all of them.

Colour

Perhaps the simplest form of magic is that which involves colour. This method of working is also used in conjunction with various other forms of magic. Colour can enhance, alter and completely change moods and emotions and therefore can be used to represent our chosen goal. At its simplest it can be used alone and in dressing an altar. (See here for some colour correspondences.)

Herbal

Herbal magic is often used alongside many other forms of magic. Used as talismans and amulets – for example in a pouch or bag – herbs become protective; the oil from herbs can also be used in candle magic. There are many different types of herbs available for use in this way. Each herb has its own specific use, but frequently is used along with many other herbs and oils to produce a desired result.

Candle

In candle magic, man discovered the ability to control light and this is one of the oldest forms of magic as well as one of the most simple. Using candles to symbolize ourselves and our beliefs means that we have access to a power beyond ourselves. Candle magic also forms an effective back-up for most other forms of magical working.

Crystal

Every stone or gem has its own attribute which can be used in magic. Crystals are used extensively in healing because of the vibrational impact they can have. Because of this, they lend themselves to the enhancement of any spell-making or magical working. Even ordinary stones have their own power and can be used as repositories for all sorts of energies and powers.

Knot

Knot magic works partly with the principle of binding, which is a type of bidding spell, and also with that of weaving, which was traditionally a female intuitive occupation. It utilizes ribbon, rope, string, yarn, or anything that can be knotted or plaited to signify our aspiration. It is a type of representational magic, and is used in conjunction with many of the other forms. The techniques of colour, form and use of energies are all used in its practice.

Representational

Representational magic involves using an object that represents something or someone for whom you are working the spell. It helps in concentrating the energy and visualizing the desire and the end result. Representational objects should never be used for negative purposes.

Symbolic

In this system different symbols, rather than objects, are used to represent various ideas, people or goals. These symbols can be personal to you, or such things as Tarot cards, runes, Hebrew letters or numerology. You will often use symbolic magic in your magical workings and will soon develop your own preferred symbols.

Talismans, amulets and charms

These devices use all the other forms of magic in their formation, but principally representational and symbolic magic. They are 'charged' (given power) magically and usually are worn or carried on the person for protection or good luck. Many are worn around the neck, perhaps as jewellery, or carried in a pouch and incorporate crystals, herbs or other magical objects. There are many types of each of these objects and you will gradually learn to differentiate between them.

Friendship, Love and Relationships

The majority of people probably first become aware of spell-making in an effort to influence someone else's feelings in their favour. While, strictly speaking, this is apparently a misuse of energy, there is a place for such spells in that they help to make us feel better about ourselves and more confident in dealing with other people. They perhaps influence us as much as others.

Attracting a New Friend

Working magically can sometimes be a lonely business. However, we do have the means at our disposal to draw people towards us in friendship and love. This spell draws to you a friend rather than a lover – someone of like mind who enjoys the same things that you do. It is best performed during the waxing phase of the Moon.

YOU WILL NEED
Three brown candles
Sheet of paper
Pen

METHOD
Light the candles.

On the sheet of paper, write down the attributes
you would like your friend to have.

Say each one out loud.

Fold the paper in half twice.

Light the edge of the folded paper from one of
the candles and repeat the words below:

*With heart and mind I do now speak
Bring to me the one I seek
Let this paper be the guide
And bring this friend to my side.
Pain and loneliness be no more
Draw a companion to my door.
With pleasures many and sorrows few
Let us build a friendship new.
Let not this simple spell coerce
Or make my situation worse.
As I will, it shall be.*

Let the paper burn out then snuff out the candles.
Use these candles only for the same type of spell.

Within the next few weeks, you should meet someone with some or all of the qualities you seek. Remember that you have called this person to you, so you can have the confidence and the time to explore the relationship properly. Never ever be judgemental about qualities in your new friend that are not ones that you have requested.

Freeze Out

There are many ways of 'freezing people out', and this one which uses ice is good since it will only last as long as the ice remains frozen. The spell should only be used to prevent harm to yourself and others, not to bring harm to anyone else. It is only used if you know the name of the person involved. A good time to do the spell would be with the waning Moon.

YOU WILL NEED
Magically charged paper and pen
Water in a bowl

METHOD
Write the name of the person concerned in the middle of the paper.

Fold the paper away from you at least four times all the while sensing the person's influence waning.

Dunk the paper in the water until it is well soaked. Leave it overnight if necessary.

Put the wet paper into your ice compartment or freezer. Leave it there until you feel the danger is over.

You then release the spell, by taking the paper out of the freezer and using words such as:

All danger passed
I set you free

Dispose of the paper in any way you wish.

You must never forget to set the other person free, lest you find yourself bound to them for longer than is healthy for either of you. By the laws of cause and effect you must ensure that your actions do not rebound on you.

To Clarify Relationships

The art of braiding is one which can be used in spell-making to represent many things. In this particular spell it is used to signify the coming together of three people and in the unbraiding an amicable resolution. In the use of colour the spell is focused either on the outcome or on the people concerned.

YOU WILL NEED
3 lengths of ribbon of suitable colour
You can use astrological colours to represent each person or you can use one colour to represent the situation
For example:
- Red for a relationship soured by anger
- Blue for a business relationship
- Green for a relationship in which finance is importance
- Yellow where communication is difficult

METHOD
Decide before you begin what it is you are trying to achieve.

If it is important to bring people together, then as you are braiding you will concentrate on this.

If it is seen as necessary for them to go their separate ways, while you are braiding you will concentrate on the intricacies of the situation and perhaps the ability to bring about open and frank discussion.

Once you have finished braiding, you have a completely new object which is a representation of the relationship between the various parties.

You should now dedicate the braid to the best outcome for that relationship.

Put the braid somewhere safe for at least 72 hours, preferably in constant moonlight and sunlight.

Only when the reason for the spell is fulfilled (e.g. reconciliation between people, full honest communication, a successful business partnership) can you think of dismantling the braid.

As you undo it ask that the people involved can go forward in life in whatever way is appropriate for them, gaining what they have needed from their association.

You may of course wish to keep the braid without undoing it.

Do not use the ribbons for other magical purposes.

A braiding spell comes under the heading of a knot spell and is a gentle way of affecting the outcome of a situation. It is, of course, not necessarily a quick way of resolving anything, but is often surprising in its outcome.

To Win the Heart of the One you Love

This is a very old folklore spell. Using a bulb is symbolic of love growing unseen and unrecognized for a time, finally flowering at the right time. You cannot simply leave it alone, but must tend it carefully if it is to grow successfully.

YOU WILL NEED
Onion bulb
Your burin
New flower pot
Earth or compost

METHOD
Scratch the name of the one you love on the base of the bulb with your burine.

Plant it in earth in the pot.

Place the pot on a windowsill, if possible facing the direction in which your sweetheart lives.

Over the bulb, repeat the name of the one you desire morning and night until the bulb takes root, begins to shoot and finally blooms.

Say the following incantation whenever you think of the other person:

May its roots grow,
May its leaves grow,
May its flowers grow,
And as it does so,
[Name of person]'s love grow.

You do need patience for this spell and you may well find that you lose the impetus for the relationship before the spell is complete. This would suggest the relationship may not be right for you.

Chocolate and Strawberry Delight

Chocolate is said to be an aphrodisiac, a mild euphoric, and helps to heal depression. It is therefore extremely effective in love potions and spells. In this spell two ingredients are brought together to help you to enchant your loved one. Strawberries are well known as lovers' fruits.

YOU WILL NEED
Strawberry incense
Pink candles
A plate of strawberries
Melted chocolate

METHOD
Be very clear in your own mind what you want to happen before you start.

Be aware that it is not right to influence the other person against their will or their natural inclinations. You should use this spell to prepare the ground for true relationship.

Light the candles and the incense.

Dip each strawberry in the chocolate.

As you do so, visualize you and the other person together enjoying one another's company, becoming closer and so on.

Say the words below (or something similar) as you prepare the fruit:

Lover, lover, come to me
And even then you shall be free
To come, to go just as you please
Until to stay your heart decrees.

Do be aware that you have not put a time limit on this so if you cannot handle such an open relationship choose different words.

As you enjoy the fruit together be prepared to take responsibility for what occurs.

This spell can be quite powerful, particularly if you use the same pink candles when your lover arrives. Strawberries and chocolate both come under the rulership of Venus the Goddess of Love, though there is a belief that Jupiter also has a connection with strawberries.

To Focus your Lover's Interest

If you find that your partner's attention seems to be wandering, try this spell. It is best performed on a Friday, the day sacred to Venus the Goddess of Love.

YOU WILL NEED
A clean piece of paper
A pen you like (you can use your magical
implements if you like)

METHOD
Taking your pen, write your first name and your lover's surname
on the paper.

Draw either a square or circle around them. Use the square if you decide all you want with this person is a physical relationship, and the circle if you are utterly convinced this person is right for you.

With your eyes closed say:

If it be right, come back to me.

Cut the square or circle out and place it inside your pillowcase
for at least three nights.

Your lover should show renewed interest.

This is one spell that occasionally does not work. It is said that Venus will not assist if there is any intrinsic reason for the relationship not to work out – for instance, if your partner no longer loves you, you may be unsuccessful in your aim. This you must accept, knowing you have done the best you can.

To bring Romantic Love to You

This spell is one that uses herbs, crystals, candle and colour. The herb rosemary traditionally signifies long memory, the rose quartz crystal signifies love and the colours signify love and passion. It is designed to concentrate the mind and to attract love to you as opposed to a specific lover.

YOU WILL NEED
Small box
Red marker/pen
Rose or vanilla incense
A sprig of rosemary (for remembrance)
A piece of rose quartz crystal
Pink or red votive candle

METHOD
Sit in your own most powerful place. That might be inside, outside, near your favourite tree or by running water.

Write in red on the box

Love is mine.

Light the incense – this clears the atmosphere and puts you in the right mood.

Put the rosemary and rose quartz in the box.

Put anything else that represents love to you in the box (drawings of hearts, poems, or whatever – be creative).

Remember, this spell is to attract love to you and not a specific lover, so don't use a representation of a particular person.

Be in a very positive state of mind.

Imagine yourself very happy and in love.

Light the candle and say:

I am love
love I will find
true love preferably
will soon be mine
Love is me
Love I seek
my true love
I will soon meet.

Now sit for a little while and concentrate again on being happy.

Pinch out the candle and add it to the box.

Let the incense burn out.

Seal the box shut and don't open it until you have found
your true love.

When you have found your lover, take the rose quartz out of
the box and keep it as a reminder.

Bury the entire box in the earth.

Because in this spell you reproduce a positive state of mind and you are
imagining what it is like to be in love, you set up a current of energy
which attracts like feeling. In sealing the box you are 'capturing' the
vibration of love and all things then become possible.

To Clear the Air between Lovers

When communication between you and your partner seems difficult, you can forge a new link using this spell, which is representational. You will need to have confidence in your own power though.

YOU WILL NEED
A crystal ball or magnifying glass
Your partner's photograph

METHOD
Place the crystal or magnifying glass over the image of your partner's face.

Because the features are magnified, the eyes and mouth will appear to move and come to life.

Simply state your wishes or difficulties and what you feel your lover can do about them.

He or she will get the message.

This way of working is very simple, but you do have to trust that you yourself are an able transmitter. Often we do not realize how difficult communication can be and here we are trying to make your partner understand how you feel, not to change them.

Herbal Heartsease

Broken relationships are extremely painful and the hurt often needs to be dealt with very quickly. This spell, using three different techniques, helps to keep things under control until you can look forward in a positive fashion.

Cleansing bath

YOU WILL NEED
Handful of either heartsease and/or jasmine, roses,
hibiscus and honeysuckle flowers
Essential oils in any of these perfumes
Rose quartz

METHOD
Add the herbs to the bath along with the essential oils.

Place the rose quartz in the bath.

Soak in the bath for at least ten minutes allowing the hurt
to be dissolved.

Remove the rose quartz.

Take the plug half out, so the water begins to drain away.

As it does so, replace with fresh water to signify new energy
coming into your life.

Carry the rose quartz with you or keep it under your pillow.

Healing sachet

YOU WILL NEED
Two 10 cm squares of red or white material
Needle with pink thread
Herbs as above

Small piece of rose or clear quartz
Small quantity of dried beans for banishment

METHOD
Make a sachet by sewing together three sides of the material with the pink thread.

Fill the sachet with the herbs, quartz and beans, then sew up the final side.

As you do so, know that the pain will pass.

Hang the sachet in a prominent position so that you can feel its healing vibration.

Healing face wash

YOU WILL NEED
Herbs as above
Boiling water
Heatproof bowl (clear glass if possible)
Glass bottle

METHOD
Infuse the herbs by pouring boiling water over them into the bowl and allowing the resultant liquid to cool.

If you wish, allow it to stand overnight in moonlight to absorb the power the Moon gives us.

Decant the liquid into a clean bottle and use as a face wash on cotton wool or tissue.

As you do so, remind yourself that you are lovable and will heal from this hurt.

At one and the same time, these techniques are gentle in their action and also offer support on an emotional level. Working in three ways, they allow body, mind and spirit to be relaxed and at peace.

Confidence in Social Situations

Charm bags are a very efficient way of carrying reminders which can add extra zest to life. This one is used to help you overcome shyness, perhaps when you are meeting new people or doing something you have never done before. It is done during the Waxing Moon.

YOU WILL NEED
A small drawstring bag about 2.5-5 cm
(1-2 inches) deep – you could use a colour such as
yellow to enhance communication
Ground nutmeg
Pine needles
Dried lavender
Piece of mandrake root

METHOD
Put a pinch or two of the nutmeg, pine needles, dried lavender and mandrake root in the bag and tie it closed.

Consecrate and charge the bag during the waxing phase of the Moon so that you can use positive energy.

Wear the bag around your neck or keep it in your pocket. You should feel a surge of energy whenever you are in a social situation which you find difficult to handle.

When you feel you no longer have need of the support your bag gives you, you can scatter the herbs to the four winds or burn them.

It is the consecrating of the bag which turns it into a tool for use in everyday situations, so choose your words carefully to express your particular need. Try to approach one new person everyday or go into one new situation, until you lose your fear.

To Beckon a Person

This is a very simple method of putting out a vibration which, if a relationship has a chance of succeeding, will make the other person aware of you. It does not force the other person to do anything, but simply paves the way.

METHOD
Say the following:

Know I move to you
as you move to me.
As I think of you,
Think also of me.
As I call your name,
Call me to you.
Come to me in love.

Say the person's name three times (if known).

You may need to recite the whole spell several times in order to feel the proper effect. You may also need to remember that a loving friend is just as important as a friendly lover.

For a Lover to Come to You

This spell is reputed to work very quickly, so do not be too rash. Red candles represent passion, so you must take responsibility for whatever happens when you call your lover to you.

YOU WILL NEED
Two silver pins
A red candle

METHOD
Stick two silver pins through the middle of a red candle at midnight.

Concentrate on your lover and repeat his or her name several times.

After the candle burns down to the pins, your lover will arrive.
It is also said that if you give your lover one of the pins they
will remain bound to you.

If you wish companionship rather than passion, use a candle of a
colour appropriate to the other person's astrological sign.

*This spell is one used to influence someone else, so be very careful
how you use it. Pins were often used in magical work in times gone
by, because they were readily available. One old custom was to ask a
bride for the pins from her wedding dress, for which you must give her
a penny.*

To Achieve your Heart's Desire

This is quite an effective spell and does give you something to do while you are waiting for true love. It makes use of candles and of plant magic. Timing is important since it uses the rising of the sun, as also is colour (red to represent passion).

YOU WILL NEED
A fresh rose (preferably red and perfumed)
Two red candles

METHOD
Find out the time of the next sunrise.

Just before going to sleep, place a red candle on either side of the rose.

The next morning at sunrise take the rose outside.

Hold the rose in front of you and say:

This red rose is for true love.
True love come to me.

Now go back inside and put the rose between the candles again.

Light the candles and visualize love burning in the heart of the one you want.

Keep the candles burning day and night until the rose fades.

When the rose is dead, pinch out the candles and then bury the rose.

There are many spells for love and this one is extremely simple, except that it requires some effort to get up early in the morning. The concentration that you put into it as you burn your candles focuses your mind on the matter in hand.

To Forget about an Ex-lover

This spell is best done at the time of the Waning Moon or New Moon. It is not done to get rid of a former partner, but to exorcize your bad feelings about them. It is sensible to finish the spell by sending loving thoughts to them. Woody nightshade is poisonous and you may not care to use it, in which case you can use a bulb of garlic.

YOU WILL NEED
Photograph of your ex-partner
Suitable container for burning the photograph
(one in which the ashes can be saved)
Root of bittersweet (woody nightshade, which is
poisonous) or a bulb of garlic
Red cloth or bag

METHOD
Place the picture of your ex-partner in the container. Set it alight.

Gather up all your hurt and pain as the picture burns down.
Feel them flowing away from you as you say these words or similar:

Leave my heart and leave me free
Leave my life, no pain for me.
As this picture burns to dust,
Help me now, move on I must.

Repeat the words until the picture is burnt out.

Taking the herb root or garlic, hold it first to your solar plexus, just
above the belly button.

Allow the bad feelings to flow into the root or garlic. Touch the root
or garlic to your forehead, indicating that you have converted the
bad feelings to good.

Wrap everything, including the container of ashes, in your red bag or cloth.

As soon as convenient, bury it as far away from your home as possible.

If you have had a relationship which is argumentative and turned nasty it is often better to end it and move on. This must always be your choice but if you wish to try again you may like to try the To Stop an Argument spell on page 127.

To Have a Person Think about You

This spell works over time. A relationship that grows slowly generally has more chance of success than a whirlwind romance and that is what is represented here. Small seeds represent the many facets of a relationship. The spell is done as the Moon is growing in power.

YOU WILL NEED
Packet of seeds of your choice
Pot of soil (to grow them)
A small copper object such as a penny
(Copper is sacred to Venus, the Goddess of Love)

METHOD
On a night when the Moon is waxing, go outside and hold the penny in the moonlight.

Bury the penny in the soil in the pot.

Sprinkle the seeds on top to form the initial of the other person's name.

As the seeds germinate, love should also grow.

Remember that just as plants need nurturing so does love, so you will need to look after the growing seeds.

It is said that the plants will grow and flourish if the love is meant to be, but will wither and die if there is no real energy in the relationship. For those who are not very good at plant-care, you might choose to put a reminder to nurture somewhere prominent.

To Strengthen Attraction

If you love someone but feel that they are not reciprocating, try this spell. Be aware though, that by using this spell you are trying to have a direct effect upon the other person. You are using representational magic because the hair stands for the person you are hoping to influence.

YOU WILL NEED
A few strands of the person's hair
A rose scented incense stick

METHOD
Light the incense.

Repeat the name of the one you long for several times, saying each time:

[Name] love me now.

Hold the hair on the burning incense until it frizzles away.

As the hair burns, think of their indifference dissipating and being replaced by passion.

Leave the incense to burn out.

Before you perform this you should have tried to work out why the other person feels indifferent and consider whether what you are proposing is appropriate. If, for instance, the person you want to attract has not learnt how to commit to a relationship, it would be unfair to try and influence them.

To Stop an Argument

This is a spell to stop an argument between you and another or to change their feelings of aggravation. You are using colour and representational magic here. So that you do not let your own feelings intrude, you might take a ritual bath first. The plate is used for two reasons in this spell. Firstly, being glass it reflects back to the person, and secondly through its colour it raises the whole question to its highest vibration.

YOU WILL NEED
Glass plate
(Deep purple if possible but, if not, clear will work just as well)
Picture of the person with whom you have argued

METHOD
Place the picture face down on the plate for no more than 15 minutes. You do not want to over-influence the recipient, so spend a few moments remembering the good times you have had.

For this reason, if using an ordinary photograph you should also be aware of where the negative to the picture is so that you are only using positive energy.

The person should either drop in or communicate in some other way within 24 hours so you can resolve your difficulties.

If they do not, repeat the procedure for no more than 15 minutes.

If after a third time you still haven't heard from them, do try to give them a call or visit them because their feelings should have changed.

You will then know that you have done all you can to be on good terms with them.

It is often difficult to get back onto a normal footing with people after an argument, so do be prepared to apologize for any part that you have had in the difficulty. Remember that you are only dealing with that particular argument, not deeper issues within the friendship.

Garment Spell for Fidelity

This spell uses the combination of nutmeg and intimate garments in a form of sympathetic magic, combined with herbal magic. It is said to keep a partner faithful. It obviously can be done at any time, particularly when you suspect that your partner may be open to temptation.

YOU WILL NEED
2 whole nutmegs
A pin or your burin
Wide red ribbon
A pair of your and your partner's clean underwear
Large white envelope

METHOD
Carefully scratch with your burin or the pin your partner's initial on one nutmeg and your own on the other.

Tie them together with the ribbon.

Wrap them in the underwear and then place in the envelope.

Sleep with the envelope under your pillow if your partner is away or you are separated from them.

Nutmeg was at one time the most expensive spice available so one would have to be fairly serious about the relationship to be willing to lock away such an expensive commodity. This spell is probably not to be entered into lightly, nor is it designed to keep someone with you against their will.

To Rid Yourself of an
Unwanted Admirer

Occasionally people get into a situation where they are being pursued by someone whose attention is a nuisance. Rather than reacting in anger, it is often easier to open the way for the unwanted suitor to leave. This spell, done on a Waning Moon, often does the trick.

YOU WILL NEED
Vervain leaves
A fierce fire

METHOD
Light a fire.

Pick up the vervain and as you do so call out the name of the offending person.

Fling the leaves on the fire and say:

Withdraw from me now I need you not.

There is a requirement to declaim passionately, and to use some force, in any spell that is designed to drive someone from you. Therefore, be very sure that you do not wish this person to be in your life in any way.

Ensure the fire is properly and safely extinguished.

Repeat the action three nights in a row.

Preferably this spell should be performed outside, but it can be also be performed indoors if you have a suitable fireplace and provided you are careful. Strictly, one is supposed to gather the vervain leaves, though with urban living this is a bit of a tall order. Make sure you have at least a couple of handfuls of the dried herb.

A Lover's Token

This bottle is quite a nice one to give to your lover as a token of your love and to intensify the link between you. The herbs are all well known for their association with love, and because of the link between the bottles should help you to communicate.

YOU WILL NEED
For each token:
A glass bottle with cork, any size will do
A handful of dried rose petals (preferably from flowers given to you by your lover)
Dried/fresh rosemary (for love and strength)
Dried/fresh lavender
Rose oil or water
Wax (pink or red is good for love)
Pink ribbon

METHOD
Crush the rose petals and place in the bottle.

Put in the rosemary and/or lavender, then add the oil or rose water almost to the top, leaving some room for air to circulate.

Cork the bottle and drip wax over the cork to sea lit. Lay the ribbon on a flat surface.

Place the bottles one at either end of the ribbon.

Gradually move them towards one another along the ribbon to signify you meeting with your lover.

When they meet, tie the ribbon round your partner's bottle and give it to them.

Place yours on a shelf, dresser or anywhere where it will not be disturbed.

These bottles are tangible evidence of the link between you and your lover. You may use them to remind you of the good times or soothe you in the bad. The ribbon signifies the link between you, so when you think of it you have immediately connected.

Herbal Charm to Attract Love

This is a charm that uses both colour, herbs and knots in its fashioning. Love is always of interest, but do remember that you need to be clear in your aspirations. Numbers are also used, seven being a particularly potent one.

YOU WILL NEED
Acacia, rose, myrtle, jasmine or lavender petals,
in any combination or singly
A red heart cut from paper or felt
Copper coin or ring
A circle of rose or red coloured cloth
Blue thread or ribbon

METHOD
Place the petals, heart and coin or ring on the cloth and visualize
the type of lover you are looking for.

Tie the cloth into a pouch with the blue thread or ribbon,
using seven knots.

As you tie the knots you may chant an incantation, such as:

Seven knots I tie above,
Seven knots for me and love.

Hang the pouch close to your pillow and await results.

This charm is designed to draw someone towards you and does not guarantee that you will necessarily fall madly in love with the person who comes along – you have simply made yourself attractive to them. If this is so then be prepared to let the other person down gently.

Fidelity Charm

This spell uses the Elements combined with herbal magic. It is an old spell and comes from a time when every spell-maker would use what was easily available to them. The best time for performing this spell is around the time of the New Moon.

YOU WILL NEED
6 large ivy leaves (gathered at the time of the New Moon)
Burin
Granular rose or jasmine love incense
Container suitable for burning the ivy leaves

METHOD
Using the burin inscribe one word of the following phrase
on each leaf:

Keep my true love with me

Light the incense and in the container burn the inscribed leaves
with the correct order of speech.

Whilst you are doing this, say

Goddess of love, God of desire,
Bring to me fidelity.

The above uses the Element of Fire. To use Water cast the leaves
into a stream or other flowing water and say:

Message of love, I set you free
To capture a love and return to me.

Ivy highlights the quality of fidelity. You should not use this spell if you are not prepared to offer fidelity in return.

To Bring Someone into your Life

This spell can be used to attract love towards you or to draw a companion closer. It should be started on the night of a New Moon. It is representational in that the cruet set suggests a pairing, and also uses colour.

YOU WILL NEED
Salt shaker
Pepper shaker
(or two objects which obviously make a pair)
A length of pink ribbon about one metre long

METHOD
Assign one article as representing you and the other as representing the person you want to bring into your life.

Take the piece of pink ribbon, and tie one object to one end and the other one to the other end, leaving a good length of ribbon between them.

Every morning untie the ribbon, move the objects a little closer together, and retie the knots.

Eventually the objects will touch.

Leave them bound together for seven days before untying them.

By this time, love should have entered your life.

There are several spells which make use of the idea that two people must travel along a set path. This one is used to signify the path of love. It also suggests in the tying and untying of the ribbon the freedoms there are in the relationship.

To Rekindle your Lover's Interest

This technique is worth trying when your lover is not paying you enough attention. You are using the laurel leaves to back up the energy that you are putting into making the relationship work. This spell uses herbal and elemental magic.

YOU WILL NEED
A large quantity of laurel leaves
A fire

METHOD
Sit in front of the embers of a fire and gaze into them, concentrating on your lover.

Keep your gaze fixed into the fire.

With your left hand, throw some laurel leaves onto the embers.

As they burn say:

Laurel leaves burn into the fire.
Bring to me my heart's desire.

Wait until the flames die down, then do the same again.

Repeat the actions once more.

It is said that within 24 hours your lover will come back to you.

Again this is a spell which must allow the person who you are targeting choices. To keep your partner by your side if they are unhappy would not be right. This spell does allow you to give careful consideration as to what fidelity and security you require within a relationship.

Resolving a Love Triangle

Sometimes it is possible to get caught up in a situation where three people are in a love triangle. It would be wrong to influence anyone one way or another, so here is a way of resolving the situation that should not harm anyone. It is best done at the time of the Full Moon.

YOU WILL NEED
Three lengths of string each about a metre long
An open space where you will not be disturbed

METHOD
Form a triangle on the ground with the three pieces of string so that the ends are just touching.

Step into the middle of the triangle.

Appeal to the Triple Goddess in her guise of Maid, Mother and Crone. Use words such as:

Triple Goddess hear my plea
I ask you now to set us free
It's not a problem I can alter
So help me now lest I falter.

These words put you in touch with your own inner self which means that you make the decision which is right for you.

Wait for a few moments to allow the energy to build up then raise your arms in a 'V' shape (the Goddess position) and say:

So let it be.

Allow yourself time to consider the problem from all perspectives before making a decision as to how you should act.

Each time you consider the position, remember to repeat the first two lines of the verse above.

It usually takes a little time for a situation like this to reach some kind of resolution, but this spell allows you to feel supported and cared for. Gradually it will become apparent as to the action you must take and you can accept that it is the ultimately the best outcome for everyone.

To Ease a Broken Heart
....

This spell contains many of the types of magic normally used in spells. There is candle, herbal and plant magic as well as representational. It is designed to make you feel better rather than have an effect on anyone else.

YOU WILL NEED
1 strawberry tea bag
Small wand or stick from a willow tree
Sea salt
2 pink candles
Mirror
Pink drawstring bag
Quartz crystal
Copper penny
Bowl made of china or crystal that is special to you
1 teaspoon dried jasmine
1 teaspoon orris-root powder
1 teaspoon strawberry leaves
1 teaspoon yarrow
10 drops (at least) of apple-blossom oil or peach oil
10 drops (at least) of strawberry oil

METHOD
Charge all the ingredients before you begin.

On a Friday morning or evening (the day sacred to the Goddess Venus) take a bath in sea salt in the light of a pink candle.

As you dry off and dress, sip the strawberry tea.

Use a dab of strawberry oil as perfume or cologne.

Apply makeup or groom yourself to look your best.

Cast a circle with the willow wand around a table on which the other ingredients have been placed.

Light the second pink candle.

Mix all oils and herbs in the bowl.

While you stir, look at yourself in the mirror and say:

Oh, Great Mother Earth,
Nurture and protect me now.
Let me use the strengths
I know I have.

Look into the mirror after you have finished mixing the ingredients and say:

Mother of all things,
All that is great is mine,
Help me now to be the person I can be
and let me overcome my difficulty.

Put half the mixture in the pink bag and add the penny and crystal.

Carry the bag with you until you feel you no longer need it.

Leave the other half of the potion in the bowl in a room where you will smell the fragrance. Repeat this ritual every Friday, if you so wish.

Unfortunately, the break up of a relationship can truly knock our confidence. This spell is designed to restore yours as quickly as possible. It does not matter who is right or wrong, simply that you are able to go forward with dignity.

Health, healing and well-being

The subtle energies which come together to give each person their unique makeup are very precious and can be conserved and enhanced. We as spell workers have a responsibility to make ourselves as healthy and whole as possible and in so doing can also help others to overcome problems and difficulties. We learn to appeal to a universal energy and its various parts to help the world go round a little more easily.

A Light Spell

This spell enables us to practice in the safety of our sacred space, before venturing out into the everyday world. It is not so much a healing technique as an energising one. The closer we come to an understanding of the powers that we use, the less we need protection and the more we can become a source of spiritual energy for others.

YOU WILL NEED
As many white candles as feels right
(An odd number works well)
Equivalent number of holders
Anointing oil of frankincense

METHOD
Anoint the candles from middle to bottom then from middle to top. This is so you achieve a balance of physical and spiritual energy.

Place the candles in the holders on the floor in a circle about six feet in diameter.

Standing in the circle, light the candles in a clockwise direction.

Stand in the centre of the circle and 'draw' the energy of the light towards you.

Feel the energy as it seeps throughout the whole of your body, from your feet to your head.

Allow the energy to spill over from the crown of your head to fill the space around you.

It should feel like a cocoon around your body.

Now, visualize this cocoon of light around you gently radiating outwards to the edge of your circle of candles.

When you feel ready, sit on the floor and allow the energy of the light to settle back within you.

Ground yourself by sweeping your body with your hands in the shape of the infinity symbol (like a number eight on its side), but do not lose the sense of increased energy.

Snuff out the candles in a clockwise direction, and use them only to repeat this technique until they are used up.

Gradually, as you become used to the sense of increased energy, you should find that you are more able to cope with difficulties and to become more dynamic in the everyday world. It will become easier to carry the light within you not just within the circle of candles, and you may find that you perceive more ways in which you can 'help the world go round'.

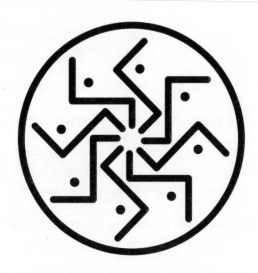

A Medication Spell

As you begin to understand colour correspondences, you can begin to use them in spells to keep you well. Many people have to take medication of one sort or another and this spell helps to enhance the action of your particular one. It does mean that you must take your medication at the times given by your health practitioner but you can add additional potency – in terms of how fast it works – with this spell.

YOU WILL NEED
Your given medication
Healing incense (mixture of rosemary and juniper)
Anointing oil
Square of purple cloth
White candle

METHOD
Anoint your candle with the oil.

Light your candle.

Light the incense and allow the smoke to surround you.

Sit quietly and imagine that you are well.

Really feel what it is like to be functioning fully.

Sense how the medication will help you.

Pick up your medication and allow the healing energy to flow through you to the medication.

When you feel it is charged sufficiently put it on the purple cloth and leave it there until the incense and the candle have burnt out.

As you take your medication in future visualize the link between it and you as it helps to alleviate whatever your problems are.

You can further help yourself if, before you take your prescription to the pharmacist, you place it under a white candle and ask for it to be blessed.

Do please remember that this technique is not a substitute for medication. You are asking for help in healing yourself and using everything that is available to you. The spell is designed to enhance the healing energy so that you can make maximum use of it. In working in this way, you will also be enabled to do all you can to make adjustments in lifestyle and diet.

Ceridwen's Spell

This spell pays homage to Ceridwen, a Welsh Goddess and nurturer of Taliesin, a Druidic Bard. She is invoked here, and asked for the gift of inspiration, called Awen by the Druids. This brings poetic inspiration, prophecy, and the ability to shape-shift (become something else). In bringing about change, this becomes a spell for creativity in all its forms. One of Ceridwen's symbols is the cauldron.

YOU WILL NEED
Cauldron
Seeds (preferably of wheat)
White candle
Incense made up of:
1 part rosebuds
1 part cedarwood chips
1 part sweet myrrh

METHOD
Blend your incense the night before you plan to use it.

Light your incense and the candle.

Place the cauldron in front of you and half fill with wheat seeds.

Stir the cauldron clockwise three times and let the seeds trickle through your fingers as you say:

Ceridwen, Ceridwen,
I seek your favour
Just as you searched for the boy Gwion
So I search for the power of Awen
Inspiration to be what I must,
to discover the known,
And to flow with change.
Grant, I pray, this power.

Since Awen is a threefold gift you should repeat the stirring of the cauldron twice more or alternatively once on each of the following two days.

When you have finished, tip the remains of the incense into the cauldron and bury the contents.

The candle may be snuffed out, but do not use it for anything else.

Ceridwen is said to have brewed herbs together to bring the gift of inspiration to her ugly son Agfaddu. Gwion was set to mind the potion but, in being splashed by the potion, absorbed its powers. In escaping the wrath of Ceridwen he became a seed of corn and was swallowed by her in the guise of a black hen. The Welsh bard Taliesin born nine months later was thus an initiated form of the boy. Artists, writers and poets can all seek this kind of inspiration.

Cleansing the Aura

This spell is a cleansing one which uses nothing but sound and can be done anywhere, though the open air is better. It will depend on your own sense of yourself what sound you use, but the one given is known to be successful.

YOU WILL NEED
An open space
Your voice

METHOD
Find a spot in which you feel comfortable within
your open space.

It will depend on what you are attempting to get rid of which spot is better. Be sure to take plenty of time over choosing this until it feels absolutely right.

Settle yourself comfortably on the ground.

Take a big deep breath and then breathe out.

Your breath out should be slightly longer than the in breath.

Do this three times to clear your lungs.

Now take a further deep breath and this time as you exhale say as loudly as you can:

Ahh... Ee... Oo...

Repeat the sounds at least twice more increasing in intensity each time until you are actually screaming.

If you can, continue for two more sets of three (nine times in all, though six is fine).

Finally sit quietly, place your hands on the earth or the floor, re-orientate yourself in your surroundings and absorb fresh energy as you do so.

Become aware of the sounds around you.

Leave the area.

This is quite a powerful technique and you do need to be quiet for the rest of the day, so that you can allow the energy to settle. The technique is a good way to deal with the frustrations of your everyday world and often results in being able to look at things from a different perspective.

Fertility Spell

This spell uses symbolism in the use of the fig and egg, but also ancient methods of acknowledgement in the offering to the Earth Mother for fertility. Crops were often offered to the goddess in the hope of a good harvest and in this spell that hope is for new life. The spell is best done at the time of the New Moon or in spring time when the Goddess of Fertility is commemorated.

YOU WILL NEED
Frankincense and sandalwood incense
White candle
A fig (fresh if possible)
A fresh egg
A clear glass bowl
A marker pen
Your boline
A trowel

METHOD
Light your incense and the candle.

Put the egg on the left and the fig on the right, the bowl
in the middle.

Draw a symbol of your child on the egg.

Very carefully break the egg into the bowl and place the empty shell
on the left side again.

Make a small cut in the fig with your boline and carefully scrape the
seeds into the bowl.

Place the remains of the fig into the egg shell to represent the
physical baby within the womb and again replace it on the left side.

With your finger, stir the contents of the bowl clockwise three
times and say:

As these two become one
May the Goddess and the God
Bless our union with child

Leave the bowl in the middle and allow the candle to burn out.

Take the bowl and the eggshell with its contents to a place where you can safely bury them.

(Your own garden is good if you have one, otherwise a quiet secluded spot.)

Place the eggshell in the ground and pour over it the contents of the bowl.

As you cover it with earth say:

I offer to Mother Earth
A symbol of fertility
In love and gratitude for her bounty

Now await developments without anxiety.

This spell is full of symbolism. The fig represents not only fertility, but also is thought to feed the psyche – that part of us that some call the soul. The egg is an ancient symbol of fertility and indeed of the beginning of life. Bringing the two together acknowledges your sense of responsibility for the continuation of life

Healing the Body

This spell works on a simple principle, that of identifying within the body whether the pain it is suffering is physical, emotional or, as is often the case, has a more deep-rooted spiritual component. It uses visualization and colour as its vehicles and calls on Raphael the Archangel of Healing for help.

YOU WILL NEED
Large piece of paper
Red, yellow and purple felt tip pens
Black marker pen

METHOD
Draw three concentric circles.

The inner one should be purple, the middle yellow and the outer red.

Add a circle for the head and lines for the legs, so you have drawn a representation of yourself.

Now, thinking of any health difficulties you have, with the black marker put a small mark on the drawn 'body' to represent that pain.

Keep your pen in contact with the paper and ask Raphael for help.

You might say:

Raphael, Raphael, Angel of ease
Help me to understand this pain please

You should find that your mark is closer to one circle than the other.

Remembering that this method is not a self-diagnostic tool at all – it is simply designed to help you to come to terms with the pain or difficulty – note which colour this is:

Red represents pain which is purely physical

Yellow usually signifies an emotional cause

Purple tends to have a more spiritual basis

Sit quietly and draw that colour into yourself as though you were marking within your body where the pain is.

Next mentally flood that part of your body with white light.

For the next two days sit quietly and make the invocation to Raphael again.

Repeat the drawing in of colour and the flooding with white light.

At the end of that time you should begin to have an understanding of the causes of your pain and how your body is reacting to trauma.

It must be stressed that this method is not designed as a substitute for medical diagnosis. It is a method of pain management which links with subtle energies to bring about healing on different levels. You may need to explore further some of the insights this gives you.

Good Health Wishing Spell

This spell is worked at the time of the New Moon and is incredibly simple to do. Bay leaves possess a great deal of magical power and are used for granting wishes. This spell can be used to fulfil a range of desires, and here is used to bring about health and happiness.

YOU WILL NEED
3 bay leaves
Piece of paper
Pencil or pen

METHOD
During a New Moon, write your wish on a piece of paper and visualize it coming true.

Fold the paper into thirds, placing the three bay leaves inside.

Fold the paper towards you.

Again visualize your wish coming true.

Fold the paper into thirds a second time, thus forming an envelope.

Keep it hidden in a dark place.

Reinforce your wish by repeatedly visualizing it coming true.

When the wish comes true, burn the paper as a mark of thanks.

This little envelope of power can also be included in a mojo or talisman bag to add more power to it. In that case try to be as specific as you can in your wish. You can, using it this way, impose a time limit on the spell coming to fruition, though it is often better not to do so.

Self Image Spell

In many ways this spell is one which is about loving yourself, hence the use of pink candles and love oil. By using incantation, you are making a link with the principle of beauty and with the Goddess of Beauty in one of her many forms.

YOU WILL NEED
At least one pink candle, more if you prefer
A handheld mirror
Love oil

METHOD
Dress the candle(s) with the love oil, working towards you since you want to feel differently about yourself.

Have in mind your ideal qualities of beauty as you do so.

Light the candles and stare deeply into the mirror.

See first the person you are now.

Visualize the change you want.

Then 'see' the person you would like to be.

Recite this incantation out loud:

Sacred flame as you dance
Call upon my sacred glance.
Call upon my better self,
Give me [your request]
Blessed flame shining brightly,
Bring about the changes nightly
Give me now my second chance
My beauty and glamour please enhance
Power of three, let them see, let them see, let them see.

You can now snuff out the candle and relight it the next night,
burning it for at least an hour.

Repeat the incantation at least three times.

*The power of visualization is a very strong tool. Each of us has an inner
beauty which if we work with it is a tremendous help in daily life. Once
we are prepared to recognize it, it becomes evident to others. This spell
accomplishes that recognition.*

Disperse Negative Emotion

Here is a simple technique for dealing with negative energies such as anger and resentment. It uses the Elements and their qualities in a very positive way. The circle of light links with spirit, the dark stone represents Earth and the water acts in its cleansing capacity.

YOU WILL NEED
A dark stone

METHOD
Visualize a circle of light around yourself.

Hold the dark stone in your hands.

Place it over your solar plexus.

Allow the negative emotion, perhaps anger and resentment, to flow into the stone.

Try to decide what colour the emotion is, and how it arose in the first place. It sometimes helps to counteract such an emotion by changing its colour.

Raise the stone first to your forehead to signify clarity. Next, place it over your heart (this helps to raise the healing vibration to the correct level).

If it seems right, use words such as:

With this stone
Negative be gone,
Let water cleanse it
Back where it belongs.

This reinforces the idea of the stone holding your anger.

Concentrate and project all your negative emotion (anger, resentment etc) into the stone.

Visualize the emotion being sealed inside the stone.

Take the stone to a source of running water in the open air and with all your energy throw it as far as you can.

It also helps if you can get up to a high place to throw your stone away, since this way you are using Air as well.

Here you are deliberately using the Elements to clear away negative emotion. This leaves space for positivity and good new things to come into your life. Under no circumstances should you allow the anger and resentment to build up again as this will negate the positivity created.

Overcoming your Shadows

This spell, which signifies letting go the hurts of the past in a way that allows you to move forward with fresh energy into the future, can be performed at the time of the New Moon. By carrying it out every New Moon you are gradually able to cleanse yourself of the detritus of the past, often as far back as childhood.

YOU WILL NEED

Cedar or sage smudging stick or cleansing incense
Bell
Athame or ritual knife
White candle
Cakes and wine or juice

METHOD

Cast your circle using the smudge stick or incense to 'sweep' the space as you move around the circle clockwise.

Think of your space as being dome-shaped over your head and cleanse that space too.

Ring the bell.

With your arms raised and your palms facing upwards, acknowledge the Goddess and say:

Great Goddess,
Queen of the Underworld,
Protector of all believers in you,
It is my will on this night of the new moon
To overcome my shadows and bring about change.
I invite you to this my circle to assist and protect me in my rite.

Hold your athame or knife in your hands in acknowledgement of the God and say:

Great God,
Lord of the Upper realms,

Friend of all who work with you,
It is my will on this night of the new moon
To overcome my shadows to bring about change.
I invite you to my circle to assist me and protect me in my rite.

Light the candle and say:

Behind me the darkness, in front of me the light
As the wheel turns,
I know that every end is a beginning.
I see birth, death and regeneration.

Spend a little time in quiet thought. If you can remember a time either in the last month or previously when times have not been good for you, concentrate on that.

While the candle begins to burn properly remember what that time felt like.

Now concentrate on the candle flame and allow yourself to feel the positivity of the light. Pick up the candle and hold it high above your head.

Feel the energy of the light shower down around you, the negativity drain away.

Now draw the power of the light into you and feel the energy flowing through you.

Pass the candle around you and visualize the energy building up.

If you wish, say:

Let the light cast out darkness.

Now ground yourself by partaking of the food and drink. Thank the God and Goddess for their presence.

Withdraw the circle.

This is a very personal way for you to acknowledge the God and Goddess in your everyday life. While on first acquaintance it appears to be a protection technique, it is actually one to enhance your energies and to allow you to be healthy and happy in all levels of existence.

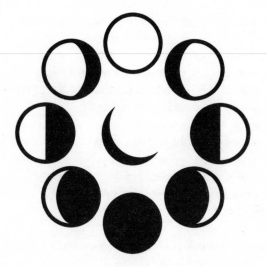

Healing a Depression

Depression is not an easy illness to handle and you should not regard spells such as this as a substitute for medical care. However, a mojo or talisman bag can be of tremendous support in the process of getting better and has the effect of continually 'topping up' the energy needed to overcome difficulty.

YOU WILL NEED
Your burin or a pin
Piece of angelica root for a woman
Pine cone for a man
Clary sage oil to dress the objects and to use as incense
Sprig of rosemary
Small dog tag, lucky coin or token
White candle
Red flannel pouch or talisman bag

METHOD
If the person you are helping is a woman, then inscribe her initial on the angelica root and dress it with some of the clary sage oil.

If a man then do the same with the pine cone.

When using a lucky token, charm or sprig of rosemary take care to dedicate it specifically to the person concerned.

Say something like:

May this token of good luck bring healing to [name of person].

With the dog tag inscribe it either with the person's initials or their astrological sign.

Repeat the words above as you do this.

Place the objects in the pouch.

Light your candle and the incense.

Dress the bag by dropping a little oil on it.

Pass the bag and its contents over the candle three times whilst visualizing the person well and happy and also asking your favourite deity to help you in your task.

Give the bag to the person concerned asking them to keep it with them at all times for at least a week.

Your subject should sense an improvement in mood within the week. You can reinforce the bag's efficiency every now and then by burning a candle for a short while and directing the energy at the bag. If you are not able to give the bag to the person concerned then hang it somewhere prominent so you are reminded of them occasionally and can send loving energy their way.

Healing Image Spell

This spell uses the very old technique of representing a person as a poppet or small doll. Remember that healing takes place in the way that the recipient needs, not necessarily in the way we think it should happen.

YOU WILL NEED
Poppet
Blue candle
Salt water

METHOD
Create your poppet or small doll to represent the person you wish to help already completely healed and whole.

Take the doll into your sacred space.

Light the blue candle (to represent healing).

Sprinkle your poppet with the salt water and say:

This figure I hold made by my art
Here represents [name person],
By my art made, by my art changed,
Now may he/she be healed,
By art divine.

Pass the poppet quickly through the flame of the candle and visualize the person being cleansed of their problem.

Hold the poppet in both hands, breathe gently on it and visualize first the poppet and then the person being filled with Divine healing energy.

Pay particular attention to the areas in the physical body of your friend with which you know they are having difficulty.

Imbue the poppet with the idea of being healed from a mental perspective.

Think of spiritual energy infusing the doll, and therefore your friend, with the spiritual help that they need.

Visualize the person concerned being completely filled with white light, well, happy and filled with energy.

Keep the poppet in your sacred space until it is no longer needed.

At this time, enter your sacred space, take the poppet, sprinkle it with water and say:

By Divine art changed,
By my art made,
Free this poppet from the connection with [name].
Let it now be unmade.

If the poppet contains direct links with the person - such as hair - burn it in an open fire. If it does not, dispose of it in any way you wish.

If you have used a crystal at any point in this spell, this should be cleansed by holding it under running water and perhaps then given to the person as a keepsake or for protection.

We are not just asking for alleviation of the symptoms, we are asking for help from a holistic perspective. You do have a responsibility if you are working on someone else's behalf to do nothing which will make matters worse for them, therefore think very seriously about using this method.

Healing Others

This is a spell using crystals, candles and incense. It is also representational in that you use the paper to represent the person you are healing. If you use an altar then work with that, but the spell can also be completed by recognizing that the space between the candles is sacred.

YOU WILL NEED
3 candles:
Blue for healing
White for power
Pink for love
Healing incense (1 part allspice, 1 part rosemary)
Paper with name of the person you wish to be healed
Clear quartz crystal

METHOD
Place the candles on the altar or in your sacred space in a semi-circle, with the white candle in the middle.

Place the incense on the left if the recipient is a woman, on the right if male. Light the incense.

Place the paper with the person's name in the centre.

Put the quartz crystal on top of the paper.

Be aware of your own energy linking with whatever you consider to be the Divine.

Breathe in the incense and feel your energy increasing.

When you feel ready, release the energy.

Imagine it passing through the crystal - which enhances it - to the recipient.

As you are doing this, say:

[Name] be healed by the gift of this Power

Remember that healing energy is used by the recipient in whatever way is appropriate to them. A physical condition may not necessarily be healed, but you may have started an overall healing process. Often the person is given the emotional strength to withstand their trials and tribulations so that an inner healing occurs.

Physical Body Change

In this spell you use the power of the crystal to make changes. By bringing the problem into the open you are creating a way to a change on an inner level which brings healing with it. This can be done at the time of the New Moon.

YOU WILL NEED
Small piece of paper
Pen
Quartz crystal
String

METHOD
Take the piece of paper and write your name on it.

Draw on it what part of the body you want changed and what you want to look like.

If you want to change more than one area, draw the whole body and mark what you would like to change.

Hold the paper in your hands and imagine the body-part changing from what it looks like now to what you want it to look like.

Fold the paper up any way you like and tie it to the crystal.

Once more visualize the body part changing again.

When you feel that changes are taking place, untie the string, tear the paper up and scatter it to the wind.

If you wish, you can bury the crystal to signify the fact that you have internalized the changes you have made.

This spell is very good for changing aspects you don't like. It may take a few days or even longer to see results, so please be patient. The spell should not be used to try to heal conditions of a medical nature.

Purifying Emotions

This spell is one that helps you to release negativity and distress that may build up when you do not feel that you are in control of your life. It uses the four Elements to do this and may be performed on any evening during a Waning Moon. It has been kept deliberately simple so that you can spend more time in learning how to make your emotions work for you rather than letting them overwhelm you.

YOU WILL NEED
White candle
Bowl of water
Bowl of salt
Dried herbs (such as sage for wisdom)
Vessel in which the herbs can be burned

METHOD
Stand in your sacred space, light the candle and say:

*I call upon the Elements in this
simple ceremony that I may be cleansed from
the contamination of negativity.*

Wave your hand quickly over or through the flame and say:

I willingly release negative action in my fire.

Rub the salt on your hands and say:

I release stumbling blocks and obstacles in my earth.

Put the herbs in the container and light them. Wave the smoke in front of you, inhale the perfume as it burns and say:

I clear my air of unwise thoughts.

Dip your hands in the water and say:

I purify this water.
Let this relinquishing be gentle.
Purified, cleansed and released in all ways,
I now acknowledge my trust and faith
in my own clarity.

Spend a little time thinking about the next few weeks to come.

Recognize that there may be times when you need the clarity you have just requested.

Now dispose of the ingredients immediately in the following way.

Put the salt in with the ashes then pour the water on the ground so that it mingles with the ashes and salt.

It is often helpful to find some sort of ceremonial way of releasing energy which enables you to let go of an old situation which is still troubling you. A good time to do this is just before a New Moon, so that you can begin a fresh cycle with renewed vigour.

To Cure Sickness
....

Knot magic is good for getting rid of illnesses; this spell is one that will help to do this. It works on the principle of binding the illness into the cord, so is a form of sympathetic magic combined with positive thought.

YOU WILL NEED
20 cm (8 inch) length of cord
Pen and paper
Container of salt

METHOD
Mark the cord six times so that you have seven equal lengths.

Take a few deep breaths and feel your energy connecting with the earth.

Repeat the following words six times and tie a knot in the cord each time:

Sickness, no one bids you stay.
It's time for you to fade away.
Through these knots I bid you leave,
By these words which I do weave.

Put the cord in the container of salt (this represents burying in the earth).

Create a seal for the container with the above incantation written on the paper.

Dispose of the container, perhaps in running water.

*The number six has particular relevance here: it is widely accepted as the number of the Sun, which is restorative and regenerative. **Again, this is not a substitute for seeking medical assistance.***

The Spell of the Shell

This is a lunar spell which calls on the power of the Moon and the waves. It is also representational because the shell is a long accepted symbol for the Goddess and signifies her ability to take all things to her and effect changes. You can use this spell for healing if you choose a symbol that means this for you; otherwise, it can also be used for other purposes. It is performed at the seaside.

YOU WILL NEED
Shell
A symbol of your desire
Fine nibbed marker pen

METHOD
To perform this spell, you must find a suitable shell in shallow water.

Take the shell and dry it thoroughly.

Draw your chosen symbol upon the surface of the shell.

Place the shell upon the shore so that the tide will bring the waves across the shell.

When the shell is in place, draw a triangle in the sand, enclosing the shell completely.

The symbol upon the shell must be facing upwards
(towards the Moon).

Meaningful words, or phrases, may be placed upon the shell also, or simply written in the sand (inside the triangle).

Finally, face the Moon and say the following words of enchantment:

Goddess of Moon, Earth and Sea,
Each wish in thy name must come to be.
Powers and forces which tides do make,
Now summon thy waves, my spell to take.

Leave the area now and the spell is set.

Once the waves come, then your wish will be taken out to the spirits of the sea.

It will usually take about seven days for a lunar spell to begin to manifest, but it can take as long as 28 days.

This type of magic is what we called 'little works' and belongs to the folk-magic level of spell-making. Take care to note the phase of the Moon (waxing for the gain of something, waning for the dissolving of something). You are using natural objects which to the uninitiated mean nothing.

Balancing your Energies

This spell principally uses the energy of the earth and of candles. The spell can be performed either during the day if you particularly appreciate the light, or at night when you honour the Moon. Often it is good to perform it outside as an appreciation of energy returning to the earth.

YOU WILL NEED
Fresh flowers for your sacred space
Single white flower
Bowl of water large enough to hold the flower
Green and yellow candles
Jasmine or rose incense

METHOD
Prepare your sacred space as usual, making sure you use plenty of fresh flowers to decorate.

Float the single white flower in the bowl of water, thinking all the time of its beauty.

Light the candles, thinking all the while of the freshness of Mother Nature's energies.

Light the incense and become aware of the differing perfumes created.

Quietly consider the cycle and power of Nature.

Stand with your feet about 18 inches apart.

Become aware of your connection with the earth, mentally reaching towards the centre through the soles of your feet.

Feel the energy rising through you towards the light.

Reach towards the light and feel its energy moving downwards through you.

Let those energies mingle with those of the earth.

Allow the new energies to swirl around and through you, cleansing, healing and balancing.

Say:

Lady of flowers and strong new life
Be born anew in me tonight.

When you feel refreshed ground yourself by running your hands over your body from head to toe.

Sit quietly for a short while and contemplate how you will use your new energy.

Finally, allow your energy to settle in your solar plexus.

This spell is designed to replace old stale energy with new vital force. You should come away feeling refreshed and invigorated. While this spell has similarities to rituals to Ostara, the single white flower also represents the Moon and therefore feminine energy.

Isis Girdle

· · · · · · · · · · · · · · · · · ·

This spell is one based on knot magic and is used to ensure that your energy is at the right level for your magical work. Buckles, belts or girdles were often associated with Isis or Venus and therefore aspects of femininity. They represent physical well-being and moral strength. It can be performed on a Wednesday.

YOU WILL NEED
3 lengths of cord about 3 metres (9 feet) each

METHOD
Decide before you begin the purpose of your girdle.

To specifically use one for health issues you might choose the colour blue, or to work from a spiritual perspective choose purple or white.

Begin braiding the cord and as you do so bear in mind that you are fashioning three aspects of self – body mind and spirit – to become one source of power in all that you do.

In this way the braid becomes an extension of you and also a protector of your being.

Call on the power of Isis as you do so to give you strength and determination

Tie a knot in both ends to tie in the power

Now consecrate the girdle by holding it in your left hand and circling it three times anti-clockwise with your most powerful hand, while saying words such as:

Isis, Mistress of the words of power
Cleanse this girdle for my use

See it surrounded by bright light and glowing brightly.

Let the image fade.

Next circle the girdle clockwise three times with your power
hand and say:

Isis, Goddess of the Throne
Protect me from all ill

Again perceive the girdle surrounded by light.

Next put the girdle round your waist and say:

Isis, Goddess of Perceived Truth
Thy wisdom is reality

This time feel the energy in the girdle and say:

I stand ready to do thy work

In future, each time you put on the girdle you should be able
to sense the energy, giving you the power to carry out your
chosen task.

This is quite a powerful spell to do. Not only does it protect you from
illness, it also prepares you to be able to help others as they require it.
Since Isis rules intuition, you find that you are in a better position to
understand pain and distress of others.

Knot Spell

To rid yourself of problems or a troublesome situation, you can use a representation of the problem in a tangled and knotted length of yarn. There are then differing ways of getting rid of the problem. This spell is best done at the time of the Full Moon and is in two parts.

YOU WILL NEED
Biodegradable string or cotton yarn
Ingredients for a ritual bath (including candles and a purification oil)
Three candles – one in your astrological colour, one black (to represent negativity) and one white (to signify a life filled with light)

METHOD - PART ONE
Your string needs to be biodegradable because it reinforces the idea that your problems will dissolve.

The string or yarn can be in the appropriate colour for the problem to be solved (green for money, red for love, etc).

Sit quietly and think of all your fears and problems.

Let them pass into the yarn.

Tie this in knots to symbolize how mixed up your problems makes you feel.

One way of dealing with your difficulties is to take the knotted yarn to a high place and let the wind blow it away, along with your negativity.

A second way is to bury the yarn in soft ground, though this method will mean that the resolution of your problems may come slowly.

A third way is to begin to untie the knots and as you do so ask for help in seeing and understanding solutions.

This last method does not have to be done all at once but can be done over time.

METHOD – PART TWO

Whichever method you use make sure you take a ritual bath or shower cleansing after working with the string.

Anoint the candles with a purification or blessing oil.

Anoint the black candle from the end to the wick to remove bad luck.

The others are done from the wick to the end to bring you what you desire.

Have your ritual bath as usual.

This spell has two parts, first getting rid of the problems then cleansing yourself of the effects. Only then can you decide how you are going to make changes in your life so that you do not attract yet more problems.

Mars Water

Water charged with iron was at one time considered to be a healing potion, creating a way of treating anaemia. Today it is considered to be more of a protective device and, when under attack, to enable you to send a curse or hex back where it belongs.

YOU WILL NEED
Iron nails or filings
Large jar with lid
Enough water to cover the nails

METHOD
Put the nails or filings in the jar and cover them with water. Close the jar and leave undisturbed until rust begins to form.

The jar can be opened occasionally to check on its condition, which helps the formation of rust. This should take about seven to ten days.

After this time the jar may be shaken and the water then strained and used as appropriate.

Keep adding water as necessary to the jar thereafter to maintain its potency.

You should not need to renew the nails unless the concoction begins to develop mould, in which case throw everything out and start again.

When using the water you may like to give acknowledgement to Mars by using a form of words such as:

Mars, God of War protect me now as I [state task]

You can use some of the water in your ritual bath or to cleanse and empower your hands before an important event. A business situation which required you to be more than usually aggressive might need a crystal charged in Mars water to make it especially powerful.

Self Esteem

This spell uses visualisation, candles, cord and colour, and requires very little effort, though it takes a week to finish. It is a spell that men can do very easily and can see and feel the tangible results. It works on the self esteem and on virility.

YOU WILL NEED

Seven short lengths of cord, about six inches long
Seven tea lights
Seven small squares of red paper or cloth

METHOD

On returning from work, place a tea light on one red square.

Surround the tea light by the cord, laying it on the red square.

As you do so say:

This represents me and all I feel myself to be
I wish to be [strong, virile, at ease with myself —
your choice of words]

Let the tealight burn out.

Next morning knot both ends of the cord saying as you do:

This cord carries my intent to be
[your choice of words]

Carry the cord with you and when you need to, remind yourself during the day of your intent.

Repeat the procedure for seven nights using the same words and either the same intent or another which feels more appropriate.

Repeat the same procedure as the first morning also.

At the end of the seven days either tie the cords together in one loop (end to end) or tie them so they form a tassel.

Either way hang them by your mirror where you cannot fail to see them.

Each morning for about six weeks choose which affirmation you wish to use that day and make sure you have acted accordingly.

This spell has a long-term effect on your personality. Each time you make the morning affirmation you are calling on the power of the whole to assist you in being the sort of person you want to be. Any behaviour which does not fit that image soon drops away.

Sleep Well

Smoky quartz is sometimes known as the 'Dream Stone'. It is an able tool for meditation, and helps you to explore your inner self by penetrating the darker areas with light and love. Because of this, it is effective in releasing negativities like grief, anger and despair by removing depression. It is mildly sedative and relaxing and a good balancer of sexual energy. The cairngorm stone beloved of the Scots, which we have seen in the section on the Evil Eye, is a form of smoky quartz.

YOU WILL NEED
Piece of smoky quartz
Piece of paper
Pen
Your bed

METHOD
When you have prepared your sleep environment, sit quietly holding the smoky quartz and bring to mind any old hurts, anger, depression and difficulties you may have.

Do not be afraid that doing this will bring on depression, because with this technique you are aiming to rid yourself of the depression these things bring.

Put aside the quartz for the moment and write down on the paper all that you have considered and thought about.

Now pass the quartz three times over the bed to absorb any negativity.

Wrap the paper round the quartz and place it under your pillow with the intent that it will help you to overcome your pain and hurt.

Go to sleep, and in the morning, remove the paper and dispose of it by tearing it up and flushing it away or burning it.

If you wish you can repeat the process for the next two nights, by which time you should find you feel much relieved.

Finally cleanse the stone under running water and keep until you need it again or dispose of it as you do in Disperse Negative Emotion on page 156.

Another use for smoky quartz is to reflect an intrusive energy back to the person concerned. If you are receiving unwanted attention from someone, place a piece of smoky quartz or cairngorm in your window and know that you can sleep protected.

To Remove Obstacles

In this spell Ganesha, the Hindu elephant-headed god, is invoked to ensure the success of any difficult task and to grant wishes. Because he represents a combination of strength and shrewdness, he is able to get rid of the most intimidating of barriers. The spell can be adjusted to encompass all sorts of life decisions.

YOU WILL NEED
Yellow candle
Red candle
Your favourite flowers
Sandalwood incense
Figure of Ganesha or of an elephant
Cooked rice
Pen and paper

METHOD
Light the incense and place the flowers and the rice in front of the figure.

With your hands together and fingertips pointing to your forehead, bow to the statue and say:

Greetings, Ganesha.
Welcome to my sacred space
With your help, all success shall be mine.
I come to you, knowing you will grant my wishes
All impediments are removed.
I honour your presence,
Good fortune be with you and with me and mine.
I praise you Ganesha!

Light the candles and tell Ganesha what you most desire.

Now commit your wishes to paper and place the paper under the statue. Say:

God of wisdom, God of strength
Loving bringer of success
Take now these wishes of mine.
Mould them, shape them, work them
Till together we can bring them to fruition.

Bow as before and put the candles out.

Repeat for the two following days, finally letting the candles burn themselves out.

Afterwards, do not disturb the statue for three days and never ask for the same thing twice.

Before long, a new way will be shown to enable you to achieve your objective. Give thanks by sharing your good fortune with others and making a further offering to Ganesha who appreciates effort made.

To Slow Down a Situation

When things are happening too fast and we feel that life is running away with us it is possible to slow things down. For this we use the power of Saturn and his control of time coupled with the idea that if something is frozen it allows us time to think and consider our actions. We simply make use of everyday articles which are easily available.

YOU WILL NEED
Paper
Black pen and ink
Your freezer

METHOD
On the front of the paper either write a few words about, or draw a representation of, the situation you feel is moving too fast.

On the back of the paper draw the symbol for Saturn.

Pop the paper into your freezer or ice-making compartment and leave it until you feel you can handle your problem again.

Tear the paper into small pieces and flush away or burn it safely.

This spell is similar to 'Freeze Out' except that we use the power of Saturn, the Roman god of Time and agriculture. By using the freezer we are bringing this spell up to date and utilizing the idea of solidifying something rather than allowing it to flow.

A Healing Technique for Someone Else

There is a whole art in knot tying which actually arose among the Celtic people and later became an illustrative art. If you are able to do it the reef knot - beloved of scouts and woodcrafters - is the ideal knot for this spell, since it will not come undone.

YOU WILL NEED
A length of grass, string or ribbon

METHOD
This requires you to tie a double knot in your chosen material. In using material which will return to the earth and rot away you must also think of the pain or difficulty as dissolving.

Tie one knot going first from left to right and saying words such as:

Pain begone
Tis now withdrawn

Now tie a knot in the opposite direction and use words such as:

This pain is held
Its effects dispelled

Now bury the knot, preferably well away from the person concerned.

As you bury it, give a blessing such as:

Bless this place and make it pure
Ill gone for good we now ensure

Now you can leave nature to do its work.

In this spell you tie your knot with the idea of binding the pain and then getting rid of it. This may be a slow process if the condition is a long-standing one and sometimes we have to remember that there are spiritual lessons to be learned through sickness. **Obviously, the person concerned should also have medical help.**

Money, luck and career

It might be easier to think of this section under the title of Resources. Most of us need – or at least imagine that we need – more money or the wherewithal to do more with our lives and the spells in this section are designed to help you do just that. Mainly they will help you to move away from the so-called 'poverty mentality' and perhaps help you to realize that you deserve to be rewarded for living according to your principles.

Basil for Business

Many Hindu families keep a tulsi or Holy Basil plant in a specially-built structure, which has images of deities installed on all four sides, with an alcove for a small earthenware oil lamp. Here basil is used very simply to enhance business matters. Just how widely it is used throughout the world is shown by the use of the second technique, which is said to ensure that you will always be prosperous.

YOU WILL NEED
Basil seeds and plant
Pots containing compost
Small oil lamp

METHOD
Place the pot and plants where they can be safely left.

Carefully nurture the seeds to maturity.

Whenever practical, light the oil lamp and keep it burning.
This action honours the goddess Tulsi who fell in love with Krishna
and calls upon her beneficence.

Note: Mature leaves can be used for this next technique. The
resulting decoction is said to attract clients and prevent theft.

YOU WILL NEED
Glass jar or metal container
Handful of basil leaves
One pint of boiling water

METHOD
Shred the basil leaves into the container.

Pour the boiling water over the leaves.

Allow to steep for four days.

Strain out the leaves and reserve the remaining liquid.

Sprinkle the liquid over the thresholds and windowsills of the business premises and anywhere else the public is likely to go.

The nurturing of the seeds obviously has significant symbolism in the growing of the business, so it is good to have plants in various stages of development. As you can see, this spell uses information gained from several cultures, showing how universal herbal magic can truly be.

Attracting Extra Money

This is a representational spell since the money in your pocket is representative of a greater fortune. Use this only at the time of a New Moon and make sure you are in the open air. It is said that the spell is negated if the Moon is seen through glass.

YOU WILL NEED
Loose change

METHOD
Gaze at the Moon.

Turn your money over in your pocket.

As you do so, repeat the following three times:

Goddess of Light and Love, I pray
Bring fortune unto me this day.

You will know that it has worked when you find extra money in your pocket or your purse or come across money unexpectedly.

In previous times the Moon was recognized as much as the Sun as being the bringer of good luck. This spell acknowledges that and allows you to make use of her power. It is said to ensure that you have at least enough for bed and board until the next New Moon.

Footwash for Money

This is a folklore recipe and would strictly only become a spell if an incantation or invocation were added. Black Cohosh is better known as a herb to be used at the time of the menopause, but here is used as a footwash which will lead you to money.

YOU WILL NEED
Black Cohosh root
Cup of boiling water
Small bottle

METHOD
Soak the root in the cup of boiling water for fifteen minutes.

Strain the water and throw away the root.

Put the liquid in the bottle for seven days and leave it alone.

On the eighth day, rub the liquid all over the bottom of your shoes.

Be alert to your own intuition until money comes your way.

It is said that you will either find money, win it, or gain it in some legal manner. This, by its method, cannot really be used to gain a specific amount, but you can bear in mind what your needs are.

Money Doubling Spell

This spell is representational and helps double any denomination of paper money that you have. You are asking that the money be increased so you may also use a herb which has this effect. You are also appealing to the highest authority in asking the Angels to help you.

YOU WILL NEED
Paper money (preferably new and as much as you can spare)
White envelope
Cinnamon powder
Wax to seal the envelope

METHOD
Place the money in the envelope, along with the cinnamon powder, and seal it with the wax.

Fold the envelope, leave it in your sacred space and say once, every day, for seven days:

Hear me, angels in your glory,
Hear me now Zacharael.
I see the need for the common good
And ask for this to be increased.

Hold the envelope up, and perceive that it feels heavier than it was.

Keep the envelope in your bedroom for safety.

After you receive more money, open the envelope, and share what was in the envelope with others.

Zacharael means 'remembrance of God' and is the angel who reminds us not to be bound by material concerns. For this reason, when we have truly shown that we understand both the value and the illusions associated with money we should never go short.

How to Speed Up a Happening

Sometimes we find ourselves in a situation that is not happening quickly enough for us, such as a business deal or house purchase. We can then use our knowledge of colour and herbs and spices to speed things up. We may not always know what other circumstances surround the problem, so it is wise to bear in mind the words 'if it be right' or 'An it harm no-one'.

YOU WILL NEED
Red candle
Fast luck incense
Cinnamon powder
Papers associated with, or representative of, the problem

METHOD
Sprinkle each of the papers with cinnamon powder.

Arrange in a pile.

Place the candle on top of the papers.

As you do this repeat the following words three times:

Time passed, time fast
Let this [event] happen

Light the incense and the candle and allow them to burn out.

A Case for Court
··

This spell should help you to obtain the verdict you wish for in a court case. It is simple to do and can also give you the confidence to face your ordeal with courage.

YOU WILL NEED
Several pieces of paper
Pen (all magically charged if possible)
Orange candle (for legal matters)
Fireproof dish
Scissors

METHOD
Sit in a quiet space and light the candle.

Breathe deeply several times to help clear your mind. Look at the issue from the perspectives of the other people involved (your opponents, the judge, jury and so on).

Try to think of all possible scenarios which might occur, being realistic in your assessments.

Write down each one on a single piece of paper.

See yourself handling each scenario calmly and factually.

Concentrating on the candle flame, call on your own favourite pantheon of gods and ask for right action. You might for example petition the Egyptian goddess Ma'at, Themis the Greek goddess, or Forseti the Norse god.

Ask that there will be clarity, honesty and justice in the situation.

Take a brief look at each of the scenarios again and write down any new ones which then come to mind.

Now choose the outcome you most desire and put that piece of paper under the candle while it burns out.

Take the rest of the papers and cut them up into small pieces.

Set light to them in the fireproof dish by first lighting one piece from the candle.

When these have burnt out, flush them away under the tap or blow them to the four winds.

When you go to court, take the paper with your desired result, put it in your pocket, and when you find yourself in difficulties hold the paper unobtrusively in your hand to give you courage.

This spell does not automatically ensure that you will win your case, particularly if there is dishonesty involved. Remember that you are asking for justice, which may involve some kind of penance or penalty on your part.

A Magical Pomander

As our knowledge of herbs and magic increases, we are able to use old-fashioned ideas and charming customs and perhaps return them to their original use. Pomanders, aromatic spheres that are prepared by studding oranges with cloves, have been used since medieval times in a practical way to keep bad smells at bay. Magically they can be used to attract money and for protection and – when they have lost their fragrance – as an offering through fire to the gods.

YOU WILL NEED
An orange with an oily skin
A nail or knitting needle
A good quantity of whole cloves
Cinnamon powder
Plastic bag
Ribbon
Pins

METHOD
Stud the orange with whole cloves complete with stems, bud side out.

It is easier to insert the cloves if you poke a small hole first with the nail or knitting needle.

Space the cloves evenly in a pattern that pleases you, leaving room to tie the ribbon. The cloves will move closer together as the orange dries out.

As you work keep your intent for the pomander in mind.

Place the powdered cinnamon in the plastic bag, and shake the pomander inside the bag until it is well coated with the powder.

Leave in a warm place to dry out, which may take up to six weeks.

Check frequently that the orange is not going mouldy, but try not to open the bag.

Lastly, tie the ribbon around the pomander, fixing it securely with the pins.

Hang the pomander where you can both see it and enjoy the fragrance.

When you come to dispose of the pomander, throw it into a fire.

Say:

As I return this to its Element
Sun, Jupiter, Venus
I thank you for your help.

Made in this way the pomander can last up to a year before its fragrance completely fades.

This pomander is multi purpose. All the components are ruled by the element of Fire and the relevant deities and planetary influences are Sun for the orange, Jupiter for the cloves and Venus for the cinnamon.

Achieving a Dream Job

Candles always work well when dealing with aims and aspirations. This spell introduces some of the techniques beloved of those who believe in using the Element of Fire, which represents drive. This particular spell is best begun on the night of a New Moon.

YOU WILL NEED
2 brown candles (to represent the job)
Green candle (for prosperity)
A candle to represent yourself (perhaps your astrological colour)
Prosperity incense such as cinnamon
Prosperity oil such as bergamot, or blended patchouli and basil

METHOD
Light your prosperity incense.

Anoint the candles with the prosperity oil from wick to end, since you want the good things to come towards you.

Place one of the brown candles in the centre of your chosen space. Place the green one on the right, with your personal candle on the left. (These candles should be in a safe place; they have to burn out entirely.)

As you light your personal candle, say:

Open the way, clear my sight.
Bring me chance, that is my right.

Light the green candle and say:

Good luck is mine and true victory,
Help me Great Ones, come to me.

Light the brown candle and say:

Openings, work, rewards I see,
And as I will, So Must it Be.

Leave the candles to burn out completely.

Each night for a week - or until the candle is used up - light the second brown candle for 9 minutes while contemplating the job and the good to come out of it.

You need to identify exactly what you mean by 'a dream job'. It is of little use aiming for something which is beyond your capabilities, though you might go for one initially which will begin to take you to where you want to be.

Activating a Wish

It is easy to categorize the granting of wishes as a separate area of spell-making, but, depending on the offering you make, it could be classified as crystal, candle, herbal or symbolic. Timings and other correspondences can be according to your wish or need.

YOU WILL NEED

Your chosen gift to the Elements, spirits or deities (this might be an appropriate crystal, plant, rune or piece of metal)
A suitable place to make that offering (perhaps a quiet woodland, a running stream, a high place, or in urban areas a park, waterway or high building)

METHOD

Before you begin you will need to have given some thought to your wish.

Be very specific in stating what you want otherwise you may get more than you bargained for.

State your wish clearly and as briefly as possibly, addressing your deity or spirit by name or title if you can, for instance:

Pan and spirits of the woodland
Hear now my request
I wish for health, love and happiness
For [name]

When you make your offering, be appropriate. For example:

If your wish is for material goods or finance you could use a crystal or coin and bury it to signify the tangibility of your desire.

If your wish has an emotional content then you might throw your offering into running water.

If your wish is for knowledge or information then signify this by getting up to a high place and using the currents of air.

You might for instance choose to scatter some plant seeds to help restore the ecological balance.

If choosing to use the Element of Fire outside then be responsible, use only dead wood and never place your fire close to plants or buildings.

Repeat your wish three times.

This is so that any negative attached to your desire should have dropped away by the third request and by then you will also be more aware of your own feelings and whether you really want what you are asking for.

Making wishes is a quick way of making things happen within your everyday world, often without having to carry out a full-blown ceremony. As you get to know your own capabilities you will be able to take advantage of the moments which are presented to you.

Eliminating Personal Poverty

A modern-day adaptation of an ancient formula, this spell ensures that you always have the necessities of life, such as somewhere to stay and enough to eat. Because it becomes part of your everyday environment, you simply need to refresh the ingredients when you feel the time right.

YOU WILL NEED
Small glass container containing equal quantities of:
Salt, sugar and rice
Safety pin

METHOD
Fill the container with a mixture of the salt, sugar and rice.
Place the open safety pin in the centre of the mixture.

Put the container in the open air where you can easily see it.
Occasionally give the bowl a shake to reinvigorate the energies.

Though this spell has no particular timeframe, the more confident you become in your own abilities the quicker it will work. Rather than using salt, sugar and rice you can use a pot-pourri of your choice. Shaking the container also keeps the energies fresh and you must use your intuition as to when they need changing.

Fast Luck Oil

This oil contains herbal essences, all of which have the effect of quickening up a spell. However, there is need for a word of warning, since many people nowadays have sensitivities to so many substances. Wintergreen if ingested internally is highly toxic so you should be extremely careful when dealing with it and cinnamon oil can irritate the skin. When it is used to dress a candle however the combined oils are an efficent and speedy way of making things happen.

YOU WILL NEED
A small bottle
10 drops wintergreen oil
10 drops vanilla oil
10 drops cinnamon oil
Carrier such as almond oil
(If you wish you can suspend a small piece of alkanet root
[Bloodroot] in the bottle for a deep red colour and extra power)
You can also, for money spells, add gold or silver glitter

METHOD
Carefully combine the essential and carrier oils in the bottle.

Shake well and repeat as you do so at least three times:

Fast Luck, Fast Luck
Bring to me my desire.

Now add the other ingredients if you are using them and leave the bottle in a cool dark place for at least twenty four hours for the oils to blend.

After this time you can use the oil to dress your candles.

Remember that, as you are drawing luck towards you, you should dress the candle from the top down.

If you are using Fast Luck Oil for a money spell concentrate on money coming towards you, use a green candle and repeat the words above.

Use a brown candle if you have a business deal you need to accelerate, but this time it is wise to add a few flakes of silver or gold glitter.

To bring love into your life use a pink candle, visualize your ideal person coming into your life and repeat the words above, adding:

If it be right for all concerned.

Let the candles burn out safely.

You should have some indication that this routine is working within about thirty-six hours. If there is none, then you must consider what obstacles there are to progress. These may have come to light since you began the spell and you can attempt to remove them before carrying out the procedure again.

Money Bottle
••••••••••••••••••••••••

Spell bottles were originally created to destroy the power of an evil magician or witch thought to have cast a spell against the bottle's creator. The bottles consist of a container, usually glass, filled with various objects of magical potency. All are concentrations of energy, created and empowered for specific magical purposes.

YOU WILL NEED
Tall, thin glass bottle
5 cloves
5 cinnamon sticks
5 kernels of dried corn
5 kernels of dried wheat (or 5 teaspoons of wheat flour)
5 pennies
5 10p pieces
5 20p pieces
5 sesame seeds
5 pecans
5 whole allspice

METHOD
Put the ingredients into the bottle, making sure the top is secured tightly.

Shake the bottle for five minutes while chanting words such as:

Money gain, silver and herbs
Copper and grain hear my words.

Place the money bottle on a table somewhere in your house.

Leave your purse or wallet near the bottle when at home so that the power is transferred.

You should find that money will come to you, perhaps in unexpected ways.

The number five is used to effect change. In financial matters it suggests movement into another phase of material gain.

You can if you wish bury this bottle close to your home rather than actually keeping it indoors. If you do this however it is a good idea to acknowledge it in some way every time you pass it. You can do this by leaving a small gift such as a pretty pebble or some wildflower seeds.

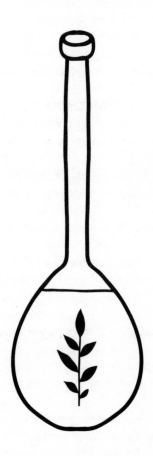

Money Charm

This is more properly a charm rather than a spell because you have formed a different object (the bag) and given it power through incantation. As always, a money charm like this relies on the energy set up between you and the money. If you recognize that money is a resource, you can adjust the spell to ask for resources rather than money itself.

YOU WILL NEED
A square of green cloth
Allspice, borage, lavender and saffron
Crystals (such as garnet, ruby and emerald or rock salt)
Three silver coins
Gold and silver-coloured thread

METHOD
Hold the three silver coins in your hands.
Breathe on them four times and say:

To the spirits of Air I say
bring some money my way.

Put the herbs, crystals and coins on the cloth.

Tie the cloth into a bag using eight knots in the thread. (It is probably easiest to fold the thread into two and tie knots round the neck of the bag.)

Hide the bag in a safe, cool, dark place, away from prying eyes for eight days.

After eight days money should be coming in.

Be as realistic as possible, imagining what you will do with the money and how best it will be used. Once you have made the bag, meditate daily on what you want. By using the three silver coins and four breaths you create the vibration of the number seven which is considered to be both a lucky, and spiritual, number.

Removing Misfortune

This spell uses plant magic combined with folk magic and the meaning of numbers. Burying an object binds the energy of what it represents and reciting prayers raises the vibration to the point where any negativity is nullified. The instruction 'Within sight of a church' suggests that the bad luck then is overseen by the Angels.

YOU WILL NEED
Three small jars (small jars such as honey or baby food jars work well)
Nine cloves of garlic
Nine thorns from a white rose or nine pins

METHOD
Pierce the garlic cloves with the pins or thorns saying forcefully while doing so:

Misfortune begone from me.

Put three of the cloves and pins in each jar.

Bury each jar within sight of a church.

Say the Lord's prayer each time you do this.

Walk away and don't look back at what you have done.

This spell can give impressively fast results. As soon as you become aware of the misfortune you are suffering, look for a common theme – i.e. are the problems financial, love etc – and actually name them in the words you use. Because you have addressed it three times it cannot remain with you for long.

Silver Spell

This spell relies on the use of candles and takes about a week to perform. Before you begin, believe you have prosperity and that you have no money worries. Consider your attitude to money. You will probably find that the spell is best begun on a Friday.

YOU WILL NEED
A small bowl
Seven silver coins
A green candle and holder

METHOD
Place the bowl, the candle and its holder on a flat surface in your home, where it will be passed every day.

For the next seven days put a coin in the bowl.

After seven days, take the candle in your hands and imagine prosperity coming to you.

Sense the opportunities that you will have with money.

Be aware of the energy that has been given to money.

Place the candle in the holder.

Pour the seven coins into your left hand.

Draw a circle with your hand around the coins.

Put the first coin right in front of the candle.

As you place it, say these or similar words:

Money grow, make it mine
Money flow, Money's mine.

Place the other coins around the candle one by one and repeat
the incantation.

Finally light the candle and allow it to burn out.

Leave the money in position for at least three days.

It is better you do not spend this money if at all possible.

*This spell is another one which is designed for long term security. Just
as you built the energy very slowly, so the gains will build slowly too.
A variation of this spell is to take a scallop shell which represents the
Great Mother and place the coins in that, leaving them as an offering.*

To Banish your Debts

This particular spell uses candle and incense magic and, if you wish, the art of magical writing. You could choose incense or oil for purification or protection, whichever seems right for you. It is suggested that you perform this at the time of the Waning Moon as this can be used to help take away the difficulty.

YOU WILL NEED
Incense of your choice
Purple candle
Oil of your choice
Rolled parchment or paper, 6cms wide and as long as you like
Black pen or pen with magical black ink
A pin or your burin
Unbreakable candle holder

METHOD
Light the incense and dress the candle with the oil.

List all your debts on the parchment.

Draw a banishing pentagram on the back of the parchment. This is drawn lower left point to top to lower right to top left to top right and back to lower left.

Carve another banishing pentagram with the pin or burin on the candle.

Place the rolled parchment in the candle holder then tighten the candle on top.

Do this carefully since your candle will eventually set the paper alight.

Concentrate on banishing your debts.

Visualize your happiness and relief when the debts are banished.

Light the candle.

Take the candle to the East and ask that the Spirit of Air acknowledges your intention to be debt free.

Replace the candle in the holder, making sure it is safe to burn out where it stands.

In your own words, ask for the debts to be banished and replaced with prosperity.

Allow the candle to burn out completely, but as it comes to the end make sure that you are present.

The paper will catch fire and flare up, so it must be properly attended to.

As you do this, be aware of the lifting of the burden of debt.

You should not expect your debts to simply disappear, but the wherewithal to clear them should come your way quite quickly. This might be, for instance, in the form of an unexpected gift or the opportunity for some extra work. Once your debts are cleared you are honour-bound not to create the same problems again.

Open Sesame

Sesame seeds are said to have the power to open locks, reveal hidden passages and to find hidden treasures. They also are used in magic to induce lust. However here they are used in a much more mundane way, to attract money.

YOU WILL NEED

A pretty glass or ceramic bowl
Handful of sesame seeds

METHOD

Place the sesame seeds in the bowl.

Put the bowl somewhere near the door of your home in a safe space.

Each time you pass the bowl on the way out, give it a stir with your Apollo finger (the ring finger) of your right hand.

Change the seeds every month, and dispose of the seeds by burying them or throwing them into running water.

When going for a job interview try to ensure that you have some sesame oil. Decide what salary you want, then touch a little of the oil on the pulse spots on your wrists. Be confident in asking for the required sum.

To Help Make a Decision
·······································

This spell uses colour and candles to allow you to make a decision over two opposing outcomes. You are in a sense taking the dilemma to the highest authority in order for the best outcome to become apparent. Do the spell at the time of the New Moon if there is a new beginning involved.

YOU WILL NEED
Two yellow candles
White candle or your astrological candle
Length of purple ribbon just over half a metre in length
Two pieces of paper
Pen

METHOD
This spell takes three days to do in total.

Place the white candle on the exact middle of the ribbon.

This ribbon signifies the highest possible spiritually-correct energy.

Place the two yellow candles either end of the ribbon.

Write the two possible outcomes on the pieces of paper and fold them separately.

Place these two papers under the yellow candles on top of the ribbon.

Light the middle (white) candle first and then the two outer (yellow) ones.

Acknowledge the fact that you will be extinguishing them as part of the spell.

Burn the candles for at least an hour, so that a link is properly made.

Consider both decisions carefully.

Snuff the candles out and next day move the papers and the outer
candles closer to the middle candle.

Roll the ribbon in towards the centre against the candle bases.

Relight the candles and again burn for at least an hour, considering
your options carefully.

Each day repeat until all the candles are grouped together.

(This should take at least three days, and, if time allows, longer.)

Ensure that you have at least an hour's burning time left for
the final day.

Allow the candles to burn out and within three days you should find
it easy to make a decision.

*This process allows due consideration of all the pros and cons of the
various options. It provides the energy for the correct decision and
allows you to be rational and objective while still taking account of the
emotional aspect. It keeps your mind focused on the matter in hand.
You do not then 'stand in your own light', meaning you don't get in the
way of your own success.*

To Improve Work Relationships

This is a combination of a candle and mirror spell and is designed to improve the work environment. It works equally well for all levels of work relationship. Often spells to do with work are best done at home and a reminder taken in to reinforce it. The spell is carried out for seven days and then reinforced once a week. Tuesday or Thursday are good days for doing this.

YOU WILL NEED
Small mirror that will fit unobtrusively in your drawer
White candle
Oil such as jasmine for spiritual love or ylang ylang for balance

METHOD
Anoint the candle.

Light the candle and burn it for at least an hour.

Concentrate for a few minutes on the image of your boss or colleague as they are when they annoy you.

Look in the mirror and visualize them being pleasant and calm.

See yourself working with them as an efficient team.

Carry on doing this each evening for a week then do it once a week thereafter for at least six weeks.

In between times keep the mirror in your work desk drawer and reinforce the positive visualization of your colleague or boss being calm every day.

You should see an improvement after a week – others may also notice a change as time goes on. As you become less stressed you may find you become more creative and can deal with other petty annoyances.

Weaving Success

The use of ribbons is an extension of knot magic and is often used in binding or protection spells. However, this one is an unobtrusive way of enhancing the energy of your business as well as ensuring its security. Braiding three strands links us with the triple-aspected Great Mother – Maid, Mother, Crone.

YOU WILL NEED
Three equal lengths of ribbon:
dark blue for success in long-term plans, and clarity
yellow for mental power, wealth, communication and travel
brown for grounding, stability, and endurance
A large safety pin

METHOD
Pin the three ribbons together at the top to make braiding easier.

Braid the ribbons neatly together.

As you do so, repeat the following words as often as you feel is right, remembering the significances of the colours:

Great Mother, Great Mother
Come to me now
As these strands weave and become one
May this business grow.

Now loop the braid around the front door handle so that anyone who comes into the business must pass it.

You should find that the qualities you have woven into the business begin to bring results very quickly. Combinations of different colours will have different results; red will bring vitality and willpower, orange success and prosperity through creativity and yellow communication, mental power and wealth.

Reflections

Chinese coins often have a square hole in them which is symbolic of manifestation of prosperity. They can nowadays be obtained through the internet. The eight-sided mirror is a device used in feng shui to represent different aspects of life and, like the coin, to intensify or redirect energy. Here you can use both to bring you tangible gain. This is best done in the open air at the Full Moon.

YOU WILL NEED

Chinese gold-coloured coin
An eight-sided feng shui mirror

METHOD

Ideally, the light of the Moon should pass through the central hole of the coin and reflect on to the mirror. You will need to use your own intuition to judge when you have the best reflection.

Concentrate on the reflection and say:

Lady Moon, behold thy power
I capture this and ask this hour
Thy bounteousness on me you shower
Bring me silver, bring me gold
Long before the Moon grows old
I ask a blessing

Ch'ang O (Lady Moon) is the Chinese immortal who lives on the Moon. In one story, she is banished to the earth when her husband, Houyi the Archer, shot down the extra nine suns which were scorching the earth. She then ate the pill of immortality, and now lives on the Moon, betwixt and between two worlds. It is she who is petitioned here.

Home and personal protection

Almost inevitably protection spells form an integral part of any spell-worker's armoury. When you are working with powers which are not well understood you can open yourself up to all sorts of negativity, and sometimes sheer goodwill is not enough to protect your own personal space – you need a little extra help. Equally as you develop your own abilities it becomes possible to protect those around you from harm.

Animal Protection Spell

When we work with Nature we are often called upon to protect her creatures. These would range from our own pets to animals in the wild and also animals that have become our totem animals. This spell uses photographs to represent these animals or you could use small figurines.

YOU WILL NEED
Two green candles
One white candle
Picture or figurine of the animal
Protection oil
Consecrated salt and water
If protecting your pet, include its favourite treat

METHOD
Light the two green candles being conscious of the conservation issues in regard to your animal. Light the white candle to represent the animal concerned.

Put the photograph under the white candle or the figurine next to it and say:

Spirit of fire burning bright,
Give your protection here this night.
The moon above for this animal dear
Gives shelter and so freedom from fear,
Draw close all spirits of the same
Come hither! Come hither!
Power of the wild and strength so great!
Defend and safeguard this one's fate.

To complete the spell, either give your pet its treat or scatter the crumbs outside for other animals to enjoy.

The animals you are drawn to are believed to be the ones who in return for your care will also protect and teach you. By being aware of their needs you become part of the cycle of Nature and of life.

Animal Stones
....

The ancients were very good at perceiving shapes in stones and wood and believed that such shapes could be made to hold the spirit of the animal 'trapped' in such a way. Many artists today are still able to do this, and we too as magic makers can make use of this art. When on your wanderings you find an interesting stone or piece of driftwood, look at it with fresh eyes and turn it into a fetish – the correct meaning of which is an object that is believed to have magical or spiritual powers.

YOU WILL NEED
A pleasantly shaped stone or piece of wood
Paints and brushes
Decorations such as beads and ribbons
Glue or fixative
Incense such as benzoin or frankincense
A small box

METHOD
Light the incense

Sit quietly with your object and let it 'speak' to you.

Allow the ideas to flow as to what it might become – your totem animal, a bear, a horse or perhaps a dog or cat.

Decorate the object appropriately, taking care to enhance the natural shaping rather than to change it.

You can now consecrate it in one of two ways.

Pass the object quickly through the smoke of the incense three times to empower it with the spirit of the animal.

Or
Place it in the box with an appropriate image or herbs and bury it for three days or place it on your altar for the same period. This allows the metamorphosis to take place and the spirit of the animal to enter your now magical object.

It is now ready for use, perhaps to help you access the wisdom of the animals, as a healing device or for protection.

Ancients believed that the fetish must be fed appropriately so that it retained its magical powers. Today, corn is an appropriate 'food', as is pollen, although you can use your imagination, since it is your creation. Should you not feed (energize) it for a period you may need to consecrate it again for it to work properly.

Banishing Powder

Most herbs can be pulverized either in a pestle and mortar, a coffee grinder or in a blender to make various powders for specific purposes. In an emergency you can also use commercially dried spices and blend them yourself. The following powder is designed to get rid of pests, both human and otherwise.

YOU WILL NEED
Equal quantities of peppercorns
(black, white, cubeb, paprika etc)
Similar quantity of ginger
Wasabi (Japanese horseradish) powder

METHOD
Grind all the ingredients together.

As you do so visualize the pest walking away from you into the sunset.

Sprinkle the resulting powder sparingly around the edge of the area you wish to protect.

You can also sprinkle the powder where you know it is where the pest will walk.

There is no need to make it obvious that you have sprinkled this powder. Indeed, the more unobtrusive it is the better. You should be aware however that since the spell uses the idea of heat, all the ingredients are 'hot' the powder should not be used when you are angry, and you must be very sure you do not wish to have any contact with your 'pest'.

Animal Protection Collar

A simple way to protect an animal is to plait your own collar for it to which you can attach various objects. Try to use natural materials wherever possible. Using the same principle as Mesopotamian cylinder seals you may like to make your own protective device, or you could use an inscribed pet tag, or a small charm bag. Choose the colours of the cords carefully according to the animal's temperament, e.g red for a terrier, silver for a nocturnal cat or a mix of colours.

YOU WILL NEED

Three pieces of cord slightly longer than the circumference of your pet's neck, to allow for braiding and tying.
A small cylinder name tag or a disc inscribed with the animal's name and address.
A small charm bag about 10cm (3 inches) square with cord or ribbon tie
Small quantity of child's clay
Small piece of flint
Small piece of coral
Small crystal of rose quartz
Your burin
Pen

METHOD

Carefully braid the cord, while calling on your chosen deity for protection for your animal, and weaving in the intention for good behaviour.

Form a rough cylinder from the child's clay and before it dries out completely, inscribe it with a protective symbol or the name of your preferred deity.

Attach it to the collar you have woven, or place it in the charm bag.

If you are using the cylinder type of dog tag, write the symbol on the back of the paper in the cylinder; if using a circular disc inscribe it on the back.

Place the flint, the coral and the rose quartz in the charm bag and attach it to the collar.

Put the collar round the animal's neck again calling for protection.

Sometimes an animal needs protection as much from its own behaviour as anything else. This spell gives you a starting point and a foundation from which to work, including further training if appropriate.

Blessing for the Heart of the Home

This is a candle, crystal and representational spell which calls upon Hestia, goddess of the hearth and home, to bring her qualities of constancy, calmness and gentleness to bear on your home. Hestia is supportive of the family and home and was praised by the poet Homer in ancient Greece.

YOU WILL NEED
Lavender candle
Small silver or brass bowl in which to stand the candle
Lavender flowers
Small piece of amethyst

METHOD
Before placing the candle in the bowl raise the latter above your head in both hands and say:

*Hestia, you who tends the holy house
of the lord Apollo,
draw near, and bestow grace upon my home.*

Place the candle in the bowl, making certain the candle will stand firmly.

Light the candle and when it is properly alight pass the amethyst three times through the flame and say:

Hestia, glorious is your portion and your right.

Place the amethyst in your hearth or close to your fireplace.

(If you have no fireplace then as close to the centre of your home as possible.)

Sprinkle some of the lavender flowers across your doorway to keep your home safe. Say:

Hail Hestia, I will remember you.

Allow the candle to burn down and then place some of the lavender
flowers in the bowl, leaving it in a safe space.

*At times when the atmosphere in the home becomes somewhat fraught,
this spell can bring a period of peace and tranquillity. The bowl,
lavender flowers and amethyst are all sacred to Hestia and remind you
of her presence.*

Cleansing the Body of
Negative Energies

This spell uses candle magic and an appeal to the Elements. One aspect needs to be noted. Black candles were once associated with Black Magic and malevolence, but today are much more used to represent loss, sadness, discord and negativity.

YOU WILL NEED
White candle (for positive energy)
Black or dark blue candle (for negative energy)
Green candle (for healing)

METHOD
In your sacred space, place the candles in a triangle with the green candle closest to you. Clear your mind of everything except what you are doing.

Light the white candle, being aware of its symbolism and say the following:

Earth, Fire, Wind, Water and Spirit;
I ask thee to cleanse my body of all negative energies.

Light the black or blue candle, being aware also of its symbolism.

Repeat the words above and pause to let the energies come to a natural balance.

Light the green candle and again repeat the above words.

Sit back, keep your mind clear and be peaceful for at least 10 minutes.

When the time feels right either snuff out the candles or allow the green one to burn right down so that you are filled with healing energy.

You should feel rested and relaxed and more ready to tackle problems as they arise. Make this part of your weekly routine till you feel it no longer to be necessary.

To Reverse Negativity or Hexes

Try this candle spell using the element of Fire to reverse any negativity or hexes you become aware of being sent in your direction. Anger from others can often be dealt with in this way, but deliberate maliciousness may require more force. You need to be as dispassionate as you can when dealing with a hex, which is defined as 'an evil spell'.

YOU WILL NEED
Purple candle
Rosemary oil
White paper
Black ink
Fire-proof dish such as your cauldron or an ashtray

METHOD
Visualize all blocks in your life-path being removed.

Anoint your candle with the oil.

On the piece of paper write in black ink:

All blocks are now removed.

Fold the paper three times away from you.

Light the candle and burn the paper in your dish.

Invoke the power of Fire and its Elemental spirits by repeating three times:

Firedrakes and salamanders,
Aid me in my quest,
Protect me from all evil thoughts
Turn away and send back this hex.

After the third repetition close the spell in whatever way is appropriate for you.

A simple statement is enough:

Let it be so.

No one has the right to curse or malign another person and all you are doing with this spell is turning the negativity back where it belongs. When you use the power of Fire you are harnessing one of the most potent forces of the universe, so be sure you use it wisely and well.

To Protect a Child

By the time a child is about seven, he or she is beginning to venture out into the world away from home often without either of the parents being present. Teaching your child a simple protection technique is helpful for both you and them. This is based on Eastern ideas.

YOU WILL NEED
Your child's imagination

METHOD
Discuss with your child the best image they can have of protection. This might be a shield, a cloak, a wall or more effectively being surrounded by a cocoon of light.

Working with their own visualization image, have them experience what it is like to feel safe and protected.

Agree that whenever they are frightened or under pressure they can use this visualization.

Now whenever you have to be separated from them, repeat these words or similar to yourself three times:

Forces of light, image of power
Protect [name of child] till we meet again.

Now perceive them surrounded by light and know that they are as safe as you can make them.

You may need to reinforce for the child the idea of them feeling protected by their own image, but coincidentally you are teaching them to have courage and to experience their own aura and circle of power. You may well find that your parental antennae tend to be alerted quite quickly when your child is having a problem.

To Prevent Intrusion into a Building

In this spell you use visualization and power to create a barrier to protect your home or a place of business. This means that only those who you want to enter do so and anyone else will be driven away. The spell can be reinforced at any time.

YOU WILL NEED
The power of your own mind

METHOD
Sit in your sacred space and gather your energy until you feel extremely powerful.

In the main doorway to the building, face outwards and visualize a huge wheel in front of you.

Put your hands out in front of you as though grasping the wheel at the positions of twelve o'clock and six o'clock with your left hand on top.

Visualize the energy building up in your hands and forming a 'light rod' or laser beam between them.

Bring your hands through 180 degrees so they change position (right hand now on top).

Pause with your hands at nine o'clock and three o'clock and again build up a light rod between them.

As you do so say something like:

Let none with evil intent enter here.

Again feel the energy build up between your hands and say:

May those who would harm us, stay away.

Bring your hands together level with your left hip and 'throw' the energy from your hands to create a barrier in front of the door.

This powerful spell should be sufficient to prevent all intrusion, but you could reinforce it by treating all other entrances in the same way and could also visualize small wheels at the windows. You might vary the technique by tracing a banishing pentagram on the door itself.

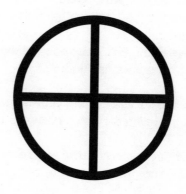

Fire Protection Spell

This spell uses the Element of Fire to protect you and create a visual image which you carry with you throughout your daily life. It requires a clear space outside of about twenty feet in diameter initially and you must be careful not to set any vegetation alight through the heat of your fires. You can also perform this spell on a beach if fires are permitted on your local beach.

YOU WILL NEED
Enough fallen wood to feed four fires
Dry brushwood or paper to start the fires
Matches
Water to douse the fire

METHOD
You should make sure that you only gather fallen wood or driftwood.

Make sure you have enough to keep each of the fires burning for about half an hour.

Taking up one of the sticks of wood, draw a rough circle about eleven feet in diameter.

Determine the four directions North, East, South, and West (use a compass, the sun, moon, or stars).

Lay a small pile at each point just inside the circle but do not light them.

Reserve any spare wood safely beside each pile to keep the fires burning for at least half an hour.

Walking to the South first, light the fire proclaiming as you do:

Nothing from the South can harm me
Welcome Spirits of the South.

Wait until one of the pieces of wood is burning, pick it up and move to the West. Light the fire and say:

Nothing from the West can harm me
Welcome Spirits of the West.

Again take up a burning branch and move to the North. Light the fire while saying:

Nothing from the North can harm me
Welcome spirits of the North.

Again take up a burning piece of wood and take it to the East.

Light that fire and say:

Nothing from the East can harm me
Welcome spirits from the East.

Take up a burning branch and carry it to the South.

Thrust it into the southern fire and choose a new branch.

Trace an arc with it above your head from South to North, saying:

Nothing from above can harm me
Welcome spirits from above.

Finally, throw the wood down in the centre of the circle and say:

Nothing from below can harm me
Let spirits come who wish me well.

This last stick represents Aether or spirit and this technique has created a sphere of energy which you can call on whenever you need it.

You can replace that piece of wood into the southern fire if you wish, or contemplate it as it burns out.

Replenish the fires from the reserved wood pile as necessary.

Sit in the centre of the circle and recognize that the fires are purifying and cleansing your personal environment on every level of existence.

Watch each fire carefully to see if you can perceive the spirits of the Elements: Salamanders for Fire Gnomes, Dryads or Brownies for Earth Sylphs for Air Undines for Water

Revel in the warmth of the fires, appreciate their light and sense their protection.

Remember these feelings for they are what protects you as you leave this space.

When the fires begin to die down, douse them with the water and bury the embers to prevent them flaring again.

Erase the markings of the circle and leave the space.

This spell or ritual (depending how ornate you wish to make it) as it is done in the open air creates a barrier of protection for you, but may also make you more conscious of how fire works. In this case it consumes that which is dead and finished with, leaving only its power in its wake.

Protection Bottle

The idea behind this protection bottle is that it is made very uncomfortable for negativity and evil to stay around.

YOU WILL NEED
Rosemary
Needles
Pins
Red wine
Glass jar with metal lid (a jam jar is ideal)
Red or black candle

METHOD
Gather together rosemary, needles, pins and red wine.

Fill the jar with the first three, saying while you work:

Pins, needles, rosemary, wine;
In this witches bottle of mine.
Guard against harm and enmity;
This is my will, so mote it be!

You can visualize the protection growing around you by sensing a spiral beginning from you as its central point.

When the jar is as full as you can get it, pour in the red wine.

Then cap or cork the jar and drip wax from the candle to seal.

Bury it at the farthest corner of your property or put it in an inconspicuous place in your house.

Walk away from the bottle.

The bottle destroys negativity and evil; the pins and needles impale evil, the wine drowns it, and the rosemary sends it away from your property. It works unobtrusively like a little powerhouse and no one need know that it is there.

Protecting your Vehicle

If you are a passenger, the first method given below is a simple unobtrusive way to protect you and your driver. If you yourself are driving, the second enhanced method may give you more peace of mind.

YOU WILL NEED
The power of visualization

METHOD
Visualize a sphere or bubble of light around the vehicle and mentally seal it with the sign of the equal armed cross above the bonnet.

ENHANCED TECHNIQUE

YOU WILL NEED
Few drops of frankincense oil
Stick of frankincense or other protection incense
If desired a small charm such as a dolphin or eagle

METHOD
Before any long journey, put a few drops of frankincense in water and wipe over the wheel arches with a sponge dipped in this water.

Burn the stick incense inside the vehicle and pass the charm through the smoke to bless it.

Hang the charm in a prominent place or put it in the glove compartment.

Finally protect the vehicle as in the simple technique.

You can expect to feel happier and to feel safer through having carried out the protection spell, but this does not mean that you can afford to take risks with your driving and you should observe all other safety precautions as well.

For some people travelling can be a real ordeal. These two techniques can protect the traveller and give considerable peace of mind during what is, after all, a period of transition. When you arrive safely at your destination it is always worthwhile making a small offering to the powers that be that have helped you in thanks.

To Protect your Luggage

YOU WILL NEED
A sprig of rosemary
A purple ribbon

METHOD
Place the rosemary inside your case.

Trace the sign of the pentagram over each lock.

Weave the ribbon securely round the handle.

Say three times:

Protected is this case of mine
Return now safely in good time.

Practically, you should recognize your luggage anywhere and if you do have to lose sight of it, for instance when flying, it has been made safe and will come back to you quickly. Thieves are unlikely to think that it is worth stealing and it is not likely to get lost.

Breaking the Hold
Someone has Over You

This spell owes a lot to visualisation and the use of colour and in many ways is a learning experience in trusting your own abilities. It can be used in emotional situations, where you feel someone is taking advantage of you, or when you are bound to someone by perhaps a false sense of duty. This technique can be done in more than one sitting, particularly if you do not want any changes to be too dramatic.

YOU WILL NEED
A strong visual image of the link between you and the other person
A cleansing incense (such as frankincense, copal or rosemary)

METHOD
Your image must be one that you feel you can relate to fully.
Perhaps the easiest to see is in the form of a rope joining the two
of you together.

If you are good at seeing colour then the best to use is
something similar to iridescent mother of pearl, because
that contains all colours.

You might see the image as a rigid bar, which would suggest that
there is an inflexibility in the relationship between you, which may
require you to deal with the expectations of others.

The incense is used to create an environment which is free from
other influences; this is just between you and your perception of the
link you have with the other person.

Light your incense and sit quietly, considering carefully the link
between you.

Become aware of the flow of energy between you and gently
withdraw your own energy, seeing it returning to you and being used
for your own purposes rather than the other person's.

(This may be enough to bring about a change in your relationship which has a satisfactory outcome for you.)

Next think carefully about how the other person makes calls on your time and energy – whether these are physical, emotional or spiritual.

Resolve that you will either not allow this to happen or will be more careful and sparing in your responses.

You might develop a symbol for yourself which you can use when you feel you are being 'sucked in'.

Preferably use one which amuses you, since laughter is a potent tool. You could use the image of a knot being tied, a cork or a stopcock.

If you decide that you no longer wish to be associated with the person, use a technique which signifies breaking the link. It will depend upon your own personality and that of the other person as to how you do this.

Visualizing the link simply being cut may bring about a more powerful ending with tears and recriminations, whereas a gentle teasing out of the link may be slower but less painful.

It is here that you must trust your own judgement with the thought that it must be done for the Greater Good. If therefore you feel that at least some links must be left in place you can do this, for instance if you would wish to know when the other person is in trouble.

Finally see yourself walking away from the person, free of any bonds between you.

Always ensure that you leave them with a blessing for their continuing health, wealth and happiness.

Now you will only become involved with them at your own wish.

You can see from the above that at all points you have a choice for your course of action. This is because each stage must be considered very carefully, and not done in anger. You must remain as dispassionate as you can and always remain true to your own principles.

To Break a Spell you've Cast

There are times when we have cast a spell that we should not have done, either because we have not thought it through or because we have reacted in anger and later realize that it was inappropriate. Then we are honour-bound to undo it. This spell is representational and the best time to do this is after midnight at the time of the Waning Moon.

YOU WILL NEED
As many white candles as you feel is appropriate
Purifying incense (such as benzoin or rosemary)
Rosemary oil
Angelica or rosemary herbs
A bead from a necklace you own – clear if possible (you could use a much-loved piece of jewellery or crystal if you don't own a necklace)
Small square of black cloth
Cord or thread

METHOD
Anoint your candles with the rosemary oil, working from bottom to top, since you are sending the spell away.

Light the incense and let it burn for a few moments to raise the atmosphere.

Light your candles and as you do so think very carefully as to why you cast the first spell, what it has caused and why you wish it removed.

Then say:

Great Mother, I ask a favour of you
On [date] I cast a spell to [insert type of spell]
I now ask for it to be removed and rendered harmless
May it have no further power or gain.

Place the bead or jewellery and the herbs on the black cloth and say:

Here I make sacrifice to you knowing that I must
relinquish this object as token of my good
intentions.

Knot the cord around the cloth, saying as you do:

I transfer the power of the spell to this object
And enclose it within its own darkness
So be it.

Use three knots for finality.

Seal the knots by dripping wax from one of the candles on them.

Then take the bag to a source of running water or a clear space and
throw it away as far from you as you can

If your first spell was done in anger or fear, then say:

Begone anger, begone fear
It is done.

You should find that you have got rid of any negativity you may have
felt. Insofar as you have given up something which belongs to you, you
have cleared yourself of the law of cause and effect and of any spiritual
difficulty as a result of your initial action.

When You Feel Threatened

We all go through times when we feel that we are under threat, perhaps at work when schedules are tight and tempers are about to snap; or maybe in the home when tensions are making themselves felt, creating a chill in the air. This spell, which calls for excellent visualization skills, protects you by forming a crystal shell around you, protecting you from the bad vibrations of ill temper.

YOU WILL NEED
A clear crystal of quartz or any favourite one that is full of clear light.

METHOD
Place the crystal where it will catch the sunshine.

Sit near it and breathe in deeply through your nose.

Hold your breath for a moment or two before exhaling through your mouth.

Repeat this several times, absorbing the light cast by the crystal as you inhale and exhaling any negative feelings, doubts and darkness.

After a minute or two, stand up and begin visualizing a crystal-like ring rising around you, from your feet upwards, getting higher and higher with each breath you take.

When the crystal ring is above head height, see it close over you, forming any shape in which you feel comfortable to be enclosed – a pyramid perhaps, or maybe a dome.

Still breathing deeply, feel the 'crystal' form a floor beneath your feet.

Conversely, sense a link between you and the centre of the earth.

Stretch your arms and feel your fingers touch the sides of your 'crystal'.

Look upwards and see the top of the dome or pyramid point.

If you can, also try to view yourself from outside the protective crystal in which you have surrounded yourself.

Now say:

Within this crystal, I am safe from negative
thought,
And am so wherever I might be.

When you feel it is right to do so, return to normal breathing and see the crystal open to allow you to step outside it or perceive it dissolving.

This visualisation can then be used wherever you are, perhaps in crowds, a sticky situation or simply under pressure, safe in the knowledge that you can return to it whenever you need to.

Those who have used this spell find that keeping a crystal in the house, office, or wherever else they think they may need protection from negativity strengthens the spell's potency. The spell to Protect a Child here is a similar sort of spell, and if the idea of being inside a crystal seems strange you could start off with that method instead.

Reinforcing of a Personal Space

In using the Goddess image as a focus this spell is representational. It uses a mirror to represent light and power and also uses numerology (the power of numbers) in the nine white candles. Nine signifies pure spirituality and therefore the highest energy available.

YOU WILL NEED
Protection incense
9 white candles
An easily held round mirror
A representation of the Goddess

METHOD
Light the incense.

Place the candles in a ring around the Goddess image.

Light the candles, beginning with the candle most directly before the Goddess image and each time repeat these or similar words:

Light of Luna,
Protect me now.

When all are lit, hold the mirror so that it reflects the light of the candles.

Turn slowly in each direction, ensuring that you throw the light as far as you can in each direction.

Then spin round as many times as you have candles, continuing to project the light and say:

Goddess of love, goddess of light,
Protect this space.

Pinch out the candles and put them away safely until you need to use them again.

This technique is slightly unusual in that you pinch out the candles rather than allowing them to burn down. This is because it is the intensity of light which is required not the length of time it burns. This is a good way of rededicating your sacred space whenever you feel it necessary.

A Spell for the Garden

If you have a garden it is a nice idea to acknowledge the four directions and to make it as much a sacred space as you can. Once the garden is blessed it can be used for any of the Sun, Moon and Nature rituals you find appropriate.

YOU WILL NEED
A compass
Garden flares or citronella candles to represent Fire
Solar fountain or birdbath to represent Water
Wind chimes or child's windmill to represent Air
Small collection of stones and pebbles to signify Earth

METHOD
Consecrate the objects according to the method for consecrating altar objects found on page 84.

Place the objects in the correct positions asking for a blessing as you place each one

You might call on the Spirits of the Elements, the Nature Spirits or on your best loved deity.

Finally, stand in the middle of your garden, raise your arms and say:

Gaia, Gaia, Mother of all
Bless this ground on thee I call
Make it safe for all within
Peace and tranquillity may it bring.

Spin round three times to seal the energy, then sit on the ground and appreciate the newfound energy.

If you have very little space, we suggest that you combine all of the elements in a terracotta solar fountain and place it in the East. Terracotta represents Earth, the solar aspects suggests Fire, the fountain Water and the East the Element of Air.

Conclusion

So be it

Holding fast to no particular discipline but believing that if it works then do it, we offer this collection of spells, techniques and information as a way for you to explore your own magical creativity. Finding the magical self is a journey of exploration, which can become a lifelong task. As always, it is only possible to give guidelines – signposts along the way – as to what has worked for others and what should therefore work for you. For this reason, if a spell doesn't work for you in the way that it has been given in this book, do try it again on another occasion and use your intuition to decide what might be changed or adjusted to suit your own personality.

There are so many spells available across many disciplines that it is only possible to take a few steps along the road of exploration with you. The actions taken during the process of spell-making become so individual that only you yourself know what you actually did to make a particular technique work. For this reason, spell-making is at one and the same time a hidden art and one which needs to be shared – an occupation that is truly creative in its output. You do actually have the ability to make things happen or rather to help in their manifestation. You are, however, never quite sure what the end result is going to be, but must trust that it will always be for the Greater Good. Someone else may well do exactly the same thing and end up with a totally different result, but one which is right for them.

The tradition that you most identify with will also influence how you work. There are some traditions that have established modes of ritual, learning, language and beliefs. Others take a more eclectic approach based primarily on intuition and what arises at the time of the spell-working. Some are comfortable working in covens and others prefer a more solitary practice. You will find, over time, that some ways of working will appeal more to you than others. Stay attuned to your own feelings in the matter as spell-making is an intimate business in which your own approach is individual to you.

As you search for knowledge, both esoteric and otherwise, do bear in mind that there are, from our perspective, certain constraints on the use of spells. In our view, spells should never used to ill-wish or harm someone – it will only rebound on you at some stage. You yourself must take full responsibility for what you do, and indeed of the effect your thoughts can have on your universe, so always think very carefully and be very aware that as you progress and become more proficient, spells are literally Words of Power.

Finally, this book is in reality no more than a reference book. Over the years, spells have come to us from many sources and we share them with you in a spirit of openness and freedom. If we offend anyone then we apologize. If we help someone then we are grateful and if others find tranquillity then 'May the Gods be praised'.

Index of spells

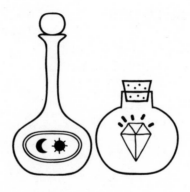

Further Reading

A Woman's Way to Wisdom – Pamela Ball
A–Z of Dream Interpretations – Pamela Ball
Natural Magic – Pamela Ball
Protection Charms – Tania Ahsan
Signs and Symbols Sourcebook – Adele Nozedar
The Big Book of Practical Spells – Judika Illes
The Complete Book of Dreams and Dreaming – Pamela Ball
The Little Book of Astrology – Marion Williamson
The Meaning of Witchcraft – Gerald Gardner
The Real Witches' Craft – Kate West
The Tarot Oracle – Alice Ekrek